CON FID AGE

CONFIDENT AT ANY AGE

*🐢 Turtle*Publishing

Copyright © 2024 Sallie Gardner

Sallie Gardner has asserted her right under the Copyright, Designs and Patents Act 1988 to be identified as the author of this work. The information in this book is based on the author's experiences and opinions. The publisher specifically disclaims responsibility for any adverse consequences, which may result from use of the information contained herein.

All rights reserved. No part of this publication may be reproduced, stored in or introduced into a retrieval system, or transmitted in any form, or by any means (electronic, mechanical, photocopying, recording or otherwise) without the prior written permission of the author. Any person who does any unauthorised acts in relation to this publication will be liable to criminal prosecution and civil claims for damages. Enquiries should be made through the publisher.

First published by Turtle Publishing 2024
Cover & Typesetting by Turtle Publishing

turtlepublishing.com.au

CONTENTS

Chapter One　　　　　　　　1

Beautiful Baby: Genetics or Environmental Influences?..7
Nature...9
Nurture..11
Environment...13
Food, Health and Weight – Pressures Begin..........16

Chapter Two　　　　　　　21

Pressures to Conform from Childhood 22
Treatments 28
Perfection and Comparisons..............................36
Choices and Helpful Thinking 38
The Characteristics of Confident People..............43
Good Philosophy..46
Living Longer...49

Chapter Three　　　　　　57

Exercise for Your Age..58
Constant Adaptation to Changing Environments 70
Positive Energy..74

Chapter Four · 77

Growing Up in a Cyber-World 78
Sharing Data 84
Parenting in a Cyber-World 90
Control of Your Social Media 94
The Importance of Safe Touch 95
Cyber-Developments 99
Assertiveness 101

Chapter Five · 109

Fear Saps Your Energy 110
Thoughts Count 115
Troubled Youth 123
Changed Work and Living Conditions 137

Chapter Six · 145

An Authentic, Caring Life 147
Your Associations 154
Post-Work Opportunities 156

Chapter Seven · 169

Factors Impacting on Self-Confidence 179
Older Relatives 193
Reflecting on Your Values 196

Chapter Eight — 199

- Unwritten Rules 201
- Rules Created by Others 203
- Basic Needs: Maslow's Hierarchy 207
- Confidence Today 211
- Never Too Old 214
- Strategies 216
- Red Hats and Ageing 'Disgracefully' 222

Chapter Nine — 225

- Milgrim Experiments and Obeying Authority 227
- Confident Rebellion 229
- The Reality of Treatment Costs 241

Chapter Ten — 243

- Our Time is Finite 247

INTRODUCTION

Ageing is inevitable. For some, the journey is more difficult as genetics, early environmental influences or fears have stolen their confidence. Our culture reveres an eternally youthful appearance and denigrates those who contravene the norm so it's easy to feel insecure about ageing, your abilities or your self-worth.

After a lifetime fearing you're unworthy, worried about becoming invisible after the age of 50, feeling unduly challenged by the changes wrought by technology, or uncertain in the face of negativity, it's common to succumb to the pressures aimed at driving you towards a multitude of services and products designed to defy the ageing process.

Following on from a lengthy career in psychology and working with anxious people of all ages, I devised the term Confidage to encapsulate a strategy for addressing the many factors impacting inner self-confidence. Lack of confidence influences aspects of your development, relationships, family dynamics, work, health, transition to retirement, and management of change, especially associated with technology and the pace of life. Recognizing you are not alone imbues greater confidence, enabling you to withstand the many forms of propaganda and make healthier choices at each stage of your life's journey.

A nonjudgemental approach, applying the term Confidage to yourself, directs your thoughts to the awareness of and contentment with the present and the many factors associated with age. The goal is to potentially increase your confidence, now and in the future.

This book is dedicated to those who have granted permission for the inclusion of aspects of their stories but names and identifying features are changed to preserve confidentiality.

Chapter One

Are we all the subjects of a big hoax by a billion-dollar industry? Can it be true that Australians spend more on the cosmetics industry than our counterparts in any other country, including the United States and the United Kingdom? Is it ego, fear or habit that drives us to buy into the beauty, fitness and health industry stories? How many of us believe we need to work at an antidote to our biological ageing? If fear is controlling your thoughts and behaviours, how vulnerable are you to exploitation in other areas beyond simply appearance?

Our language is peppered with rhetoric about how each decade makes us younger.

We've been told 'sixty is the new forty' or 'forty is the new twenty'. We're led to expect that a youthful appearance, slim, toned body, and filling ourselves with additional vitamins and supplements will enhance our confidence, make us more popular, help us obtain or keep a job and retain longer life.

I knew from a lifetime of working with vulnerable people of all ages that self-doubt saps confidence. In my day-to-day work at a medical centre, I became increasingly aware that people from all walks of life and across all age groups were turning to the cosmetic industry in the belief that enhancement of their physical characteristics would result in increased confidence. Their stories prompted me to investigate the extent to which people would go, despite the costs, to change their bodies as a means of achieving self-esteem.

I found those whose confidence was limited by downplaying their achievements while equating success with body enhancements. Males and female clients, young and old, with low self-esteem and no financial security, proudly displayed discreet and not-so-subtle tattoos and other body markings. They explained that it was a measure of their success, demonstrating their strength or 'art'.

Many clients who lacked confidence focussed on decorating or changing their bodies through various enhancements. I sought to understand this emphasis on looks. It was often described by young people as a response to peer pressure. Many did not realise the subtle propaganda and other pressures in force, destroying their inner self-assurance.

The more I focussed on lack of confidence, the greater my realisation that it's wide-spread among all age groups as demonstrated to me at a businesswomen's lunch. I chatted with my neighbour, a well-dressed, successful woman, who revealed her relief at the recent sale of her business for a huge profit to an overseas company. She then enquired around the table to see if anyone could offer recommendations for a good cosmetic dental surgeon because she habitually ground her teeth when stressed.

I was surprised that, with her newly acquired wealth, her first priority was to have *all* her teeth capped or crowned. I was sad to hear that this obviously competent woman was so stressed. I was also confused that she was still so insecure that her first priority, having sold her business, was to change her appearance.

Continuing our conversation, she complained that she had friends who 'can afford to do something about all their lines but don't'. In her view, it was incumbent on women with time and the means to undertake all that cosmetic surgery has to offer. Hence her plans to use her newly acquired free time to work on her appearance, beginning with her teeth.

This woman seemed so unhappy about the way she looked, yet I saw a well-groomed woman with beautiful skin and a trim figure. When I said as much, she negated my compliments, explaining that although she maintained her weight by having regular gym sessions with her personal trainer before work, she was becoming unhappy with him. I noticed she only picked at a tiny amount of the food placed before us. Despite her achievements, it was obvious that she lacked confidence.

Coincidentally, I met up with the same woman some months later. Her mouth was a dazzling display of white, well-formed teeth. I also noted that her face was plumper, her skin was taut and she was just as thin. She flippantly dismissed my remarks about finding a dental surgeon and talked instead about the marvellous new plastic surgeon she'd discovered, the cosmetic procedures available and his surgical skills.

Whereas once she'd used mountains of energy to create a business empire, she was becoming addicted to a new sort of busy-ness instead. Without her former business to work on and with nothing else to replace it, her new project involved working on her physical appearance.

Not everyone has that level of financial security, yet I had female clients who used up all their savings on breast augmentation at the behest of their boyfriends. Also, young men, equally impoverished, who revealed the results of expensive cosmetic procedures including abdominal reshaping and liposuction to alter and reshape their chests. They proudly displayed their six-pack abs and didn't baulk when reporting to me that the procedures could cost more than $10,000. It was an exorbitant cost for low-paid and under-employed men and I wondered how they could afford it but without prompting, I learnt that some flew to Bali to get treatments and dental procedures as at that time it was cheaper. Others said they'd travelled to Asia where cosmetic procedures were cheaper than in Australia.

Walking to work, I began to take notice of signs for treatments in the windows of the beauty salons I passed. I wondered how so many people could be so insecure that they afforded themselves procedures reaching thousands of dollars. These costs seemed prohibitive to me. I found it difficult to understand why the cost wasn't a deterrent to my clients.

In my professional capacity and as a parent and friend, my attention was directed to people's focus on appearance, so I decided on a new approach. I wanted to help people achieve inner confidence without resorting to changing their appearance. I determined to assist people to acknowledge their true worth by understanding and accepting themselves unconditionally.

Reflecting on my experience with that businesswoman, as well as other acquaintances, and my many clients with low self-esteem, I devised the term 'Confidage'. By using a label, clients, colleagues, family and friends reported feeling empowered. They noted that identifying their actions led to changes and in the process, they gained (or re-gained) confidence without turning to artifice.

My goal in creating the term resulted in providing an umbrella under which everyone could explore, challenge, question and discover new strategies to heighten their self-awareness and expand their confidence. Feedback revealed that by embracing the terminology, people felt empowered to speak out and withstand clever marketing, propaganda and peer pressure.

Reflecting on the influences on their lives, they no longer blindly conformed to an artificially devised, idealised appearance. They began to make more helpful conscious choices in the face of a myriad of challenges associated with chronological ageing.

Many of their personal stories are shared here. Their narratives are offered so you can consciously and confidently manage transitions in your life. We begin by understanding how confidence develops due to the influence of genetics and the environment on your thoughts and behaviours.

Beautiful Baby: Genetics or Environmental Influences?

Most babies are born beautiful, especially if you speak to adoring new parents. Well-formed, soft skin, smelling sweet with an innocent smile, newborns are eye-catching. Who isn't entranced by a new baby, little kittens, small puppies or baby chickens? There's something vulnerable and endearing about tiny helpless creatures that bring out our urge to protect them. They unconditionally offer signs of affection. Faced with their non-judgemental responses, it's easy to feel calmly confident in their presence, unconcerned about appearance, thoughts or actions.

Cute and cuddly as a baby, how is it that as we develop, self-doubt about our appearance or achievements has the potential to cripple our self-confidence? When you think about your own confidence, are you conscious that it has partially disappeared? Did you lose it due to the type of nurturing and modelling you experienced in your formative years? Or was the development of your self-confidence shaped by the natural characteristics you inherited from your parents?

You have little say over traits inherited from biological parents. From eye colour to skin type and body shape, aspects of your nature and automatic responses, even your athletic abilities, these are all things you inherited from them. Some characteristics you may wish to ditch or attempt to alter, especially appearance, yet you might remain largely unaware of other inherited traits until you catch yourself sounding or behaving just like one of your parents.

The environment we are born into influences each of us differently, as do factors such as our position in the family. You'll be aware of the different treatment and behaviours of the first-born, middle child or baby of the family. Although traits are inherited, your place in the family impacts your development and how others treat you, as does the environment you inhabited as a child.

Even before birth, your mother's health during pregnancy also played a role in your progress. In the past, women were unaware of the effects on the developing foetus of smoking during pregnancy or the influence of their alcohol intake on an unborn baby. Smoking was commonplace.

Today's mothers are more aware of all these influences. Wanting a healthy pregnancy, they're mindful of not smoking. They avoid alcohol and search multiple sources of information about what foods to eat and to avoid. Our systems also offer medical care to ensure the optimal development of a healthy baby.

Social scientists research whether or not it's the world we are born into and the nurturing that we experience or our inherited characteristics that shape our behaviour. This nature/nurture debate continues. I argue that both play an important role in the development of your self-confidence.

Nature

It's natural to enjoy babies. Small, helpless, defenseless, babies' eyes shine brightly in readiness to absorb the world around them. They come to know the world through poking, pulling and tasting everything. They gurgle happily when sated and clean or cry to alert an adult to their needs if they're uncomfortable.

Babies instinctively smile, then when a parent/caregiver or other person smiles in return, they begin to learn about emotions. Their inherent natural skills include motor skills, enabling them to grasp a rattle. This biosocial development is pre-programmed.

This is how you subliminally learnt things. You absorbed behaviours as diverse as risk-taking through to a myriad of differing attitudes that guide your approaches and reactions in life. If you've ever done a personality test you may have identified the inherited aspects of your nature.

Do you recognise that your cognitive capacity is the same as one of your parents? Maybe you were born with a phenomenal memory and/or you know other family members to whom this inherited characteristic applies. Perhaps you inherited a creative imagination or a particular aptitude for languages. There are as many patterns of development as there are individuals, so no two people (with the exception of twins), despite growing up in the same family, look or behave in the same way. Yet you will see from family photographs how DNA has shaped appearances across multiple generations. What you can't see is what they say, how they behave and why.

Traits may be inherited from your biological parents, but life's experiences frame your views. You may try to consciously change, whilst others remain unaware of the extent to which perceptions and actions in life are linked to heredity (nature) and environment (nurture).

Nurture

Babies, at the centre of their family's universe, learn that crying results in being picked up. Thus, they trust that their needs will be met. When they smile, people smile back and they learn to repeat it to be rewarded. Who hasn't responded to the baby throwing a toy on the floor? When you pick it up and return it, they'll do it again, confident of your response.

All humans require someone to provide adequate shelter, security and food. When you were small, you relied on parents or caregivers to take care of these basic needs. Emotional behaviours are also influenced and shaped by your environment.

Positive acclamations from proud parents and relatives and friends, exclaiming in amazement as you reached each developmental milestone, laid a solid foundation for building your self-confidence. Observers' comments about your smile or physical features, or their reflections on your capabilities, whilst not able to be processed cognitively when you were a baby due to the absence of language skills, were nevertheless absorbed as feelings.

Moving from babyhood to becoming a toddler, you started the separation process. From total dependence on a caregiver, you learnt to explore the environment. You learnt resilience first by crawling, then by taking a few tentative steps and stumbling.

Attachment and dependence on your caregiver changed as you mastered walking. Your growth and advancement were also subject to the social mores of the society, community and culture into which you were born.

If as a baby you grew up in a loving and protected environment where people spoke freely and acted lovingly towards each other, each new experience engendered confidence. Sadly, not everyone is nurtured ideally. For some, familial relationships are abusive. It requires strength to overcome such adversity and to maintain self-esteem. The absence of nurturing means learning about feelings differently.

As a toddler, you internalised the images and mannerisms of those who populated your world whilst running around and exploring an expanding environment. A natural phase of learning for toddlers (and teens) is to seek out and challenge boundaries. You may recall becoming so independent you tried to shake off your parent's hand as they guided you across the street.

Parents encourage mastery of new physical and mental skills. In addition to being busy physically exploring the world, the brain is absorbing masses of data. Remember as a toddler trying to walk in your mother's shoes, parading around the place to the delighted laughter of siblings or other adults? Maybe you were the child who stood at the basin, curiously watching your father while he was shaving before going to work. The subliminal message it taught you was that the people you cared for would leave, but they would return.

Parenting involves creating the child's environment as well as providing a genetic inheritance. The responses of adults in their environment either piques the child's innate or learned curiosity or enhances fear. Toddlers who absorb fear and anxiety may hold it for their lifetime.

Environment

As a social species, we need strong relationships in order to flourish. We grow through experiencing healthy interactions among families, friends, groups, neighbours and the wider community. But mobility is the norm today and moving home regularly leads to social fragmentation.

People are too busy to chat over the fence or stop halfway up the stairs to say hello as in bygone days, nor do they drop in unannounced. They rush into their garages or apartments and lock the doors. Social events are more likely to occur over coffee or wine at a café or restaurant than in the home. This lack of connectivity does little to sustain us or assist us in building confidence.

Service providers mind the children and it's likely that we hardly know our neighbours. Children can bear the brunt of this disconnect, with increasing levels of fear and distrust.

Their world is different from the one your parents and grandparents experienced. Since the introduction of widespread television viewing, advertisers and aspects of the media subliminally shaped our culture.

Today many children are confined indoors, reliant on media for entertainment. It's difficult to monitor their viewing as it's used widely in schools, among friends and in the home. Confronted by imagery 24/7 through public and social media, we don't yet understand how it affects physical and language development, aggression, social interaction or self-confidence.

Focused on physical appearance, young children may be intrigued by watching televised images of people in costumes. Alternatively, it may scare them, especially when someone looks markedly different.

In bygone days, there was less publicity about the abuse of children. Now society is more aware of the potential for negative or abusive interactions emanating from a trusted adult figure, even one dressed as Santa. Sitting on the knee of a man dressed up in costume is now banned.

This level of distrust has expanded to include family figures such as uncles and grandfathers because of negative experiences between children and adults. If not reported or supported, these behaviours can have a devasting and lifelong impact on trust and confidence.

Maybe you felt fear when you were teased by older siblings or by callers arriving at your door dressed in Halloween costumes. Unresolved, even unacknowledged, such fears can be at the core of fear and low self-esteem through to adulthood.

Genetics, diet, family and environmental influences, drugs and cognitive mastery impact our sense of competence as we move through life stages. Physiological changes, moving to a new suburb and/or school, a desire to conform, and genetics or family modelling may predispose children to anxiety.

Lack of social cohesion impacts all generations. Isolation deprives children, youth and adults of confidence. It can lead to people feeling nervous, excluded, ignored and underappreciated.

The advent of busy two-parent working lifestyles that results in changes to family diets and eating habits, may also contribute to a lack of confidence. Meal preparations and behaviours revolve around the ease of access to fast food and the influence of advertised junk food alternatives. Less fresh food, more packaged products and limited time to prepare meals have wrought less nutritional health. The result can leave children feeling that the only thing they can control is what they put into their bodies.

Food, Health and Weight – Pressures Begin

Physical changes begin in childhood between the ages of eight to twelve, a time referred to as the tweens. At that stage, coinciding with bodily transformation, they move away from their parents towards independence.

But even tweens obsess about their appearance, as well as food and body shape. They may overeat for comfort, or at the other extreme, starve themselves. Neither are healthy. Being overweight can impose stress on the body and starvation is especially damaging to young bodies, which need adequate nutrition to thrive.

The risks to health increase through the teenage years. This is an especially challenging time as the focus is on gaining peer acceptance while bodies are changing biologically. Interactions with family members decline because teenagers spend more time with peers. Seeking validation as well as companionship may induce vulnerability to mental health issues including body dysmorphia.

The COVID-19 pandemic contributed to mental health conditions including eating disorders. For vulnerable people of all ages, being locked in their homes and more frequently, seeing themselves on a screen, fed an unhealthy obsession about even minor flaws in their appearance.

The social world for children and young people locked out of their social and educational worlds, banned from going outside in some states for more than an hour a day for exercise, was limited to technology. Pandemic rules precluded young people from socialising, engaging in sport, or going out shopping. It impacted on their schooling, as their only option for academic engagement was online.

Body image crises keeping children and youth out of school is not a new phenomenon. Research by The Butterfly Foundation indicates that nearly half of high school students have skipped school due to poor body image.

Eating disorders flourish in a culture when we think we're expected to look a certain way. Family, teachers, peers, colleagues, partners and people in your social group can positively influence your sense of confidence. However, when the tape playing in your head is a silent 'you have to become thinner', it's easy to equate negativity about body shape and size with unworthiness. The emphasis on the body among athletes, models and people whose work or sport demands a particular physique has been associated with the subsequent development of an eating disorder.

The media may offer a distraction from uncomfortable feelings and mask anxiety and stressors in the immediate environment, but it also fuels insecurity. Separation from other flesh and blood human beings, only sharing with them electronically via a plastic screen, is not the answer.

Following social media influencers, those whose incomes are derived from showing off various 'ideal' body images, does nothing to enhance your positive feelings. Yet despite teasing or negative comments about their appearance, three-quarters of young people never take a break from social media.

Eating disorders are likely to begin in adolescence among females, and later in males. Girls and women may think they can't wear certain items of clothing because in their minds or due to comments however innocent or well-intended, they think they'll look too fat. For the female or male with low self-esteem, perfectionist tendencies and/or who has been bullied about weight or their body, such comments can begin a spiral into negative actions.

Disordered eating behaviours in boys and men present differently. Their ideal image centres on developing a muscular and lean physique, rather than focussing on weight. They're more likely to be preoccupied with fitness, engaging in constant and repetitive dieting, and may turn to muscle-enhancing drugs.

Body image can affect people of all ages and across all cultures. Maybe you became unhappy with your post-pregnancy shape or changes as you are ageing. You may automatically activate these negative habitual messages or resume unhealthy food habits as an adult when you're busy and overly stressed.

The good news is that once you consciously monitor your stress level, you can do something about it before any disturbing thoughts reach an unworkable extent and you revert to unhelpful behaviours.

Chapter Two

The concept of ageing gracefully has all but disappeared from our lexicon. The alternative viewpoint promulgated is to remain forever young. You must supposedly change something such as your skin or body shape so you look younger, trimmer or more muscular, then, in turn, you'll be more comfortable among your peers, at work or have greater success in relationships. It's easy to be seduced by the idea that you *must* be happy and that happiness is associated with being attractive and young.

The King of Pop, the now-deceased musician and entertainer Michael Jackson was so unhappy and troubled by his appearance that he surgically altered his features and even his skin. Television programs add to the pressures by reinforcing an emphasis on skin tone. In one example, contestants are sprayed with a tanning product to change the colour of their skin. In other cultures, individuals with different skin tones aim for whiter skin.

Are we being manipulated by an industry urging conformity to some idealised and/or unachievable norm? Even models, famed for their beauty, obsess over minor flaws. Being insecure, they are likely to seek happiness by making even small changes such as the size or shape of their nose or eyelids.

Beauty and ageing are complex. However, genetics cannot be altered. Ageing, a physiological process for our physical bodies, is also psychologically complicated. From young girls to older males, none are immune to the pressures. Everyone manages chronological development differently. Genetics and our environment impact on confidence at each and every age and stage of life but it's not correlated with age.

Pressures to Conform from Childhood

Life stages follow similar patterns in the western world. First a student, then self-supporting through work, you move through yet another phase of life if you marry and/or raise a family. Then it's forward towards retirement.

Advertisers are so adept at coercion that from the earliest of ages, even as a young child, you probably bought into the hype around the necessity of having certain material possessions. Babies sitting in their prams glued to mobile phones are already subliminally desensitised. Everything from material goods to behaviours showcasing what people look like, how they speak, say and do and what they need, all are cleverly contained in a catchy cartoon format.

By the time they reach school age, children are aware of physical, pecuniary and other differences between people largely due to having unintentionally absorbed media imagery from the advertisements in their constant media viewing. For example, as our governments and banks emphasise and ensure the ease of digital currency, they're rarely exposed to cash. Thus, they're unlikely to understand the value of actual physical money and how finances relate to purchasing power.

Advertising, media messaging and listening in on adult's conversations ensures children are more likely to recognise fashion labels, brand names, more expensive cars and the cost and size of houses. Constantly viewing YouTube or other media in their living rooms, on their tablets and iPhones, regularly shopping, or comparing their possessions with their peers, children's confidence can be built or destroyed, often without their parents' awareness.

Due to the emphasis on consumption by the media, financial considerations, wealth and our banking system are beyond their knowledge. Authors such as Robert T Kiyosaki, who wrote *Rich Dad Poor Dad for Teens: The Secrets about Money That You Don't Learn in School!* addresses this by prescribing lessons relating to money and smart choices. His books provide valuable lessons about overcoming fear, self-doubt and limiting beliefs, in this case, about money.

In *The Barefoot Investor*, Scott Pape outlines steps for financial literacy. He suggests putting 50% of your money towards things you need, 30% to wants and saving 20% so that you have the money to realise future goals. This advice can habituate anyone into saving a portion of their income for their future, whereas credit cards, computer chips, AI and the phenomena of tapping a phone to purchase products as basic as foodstuffs make it too easy not to think.

The concept of financial reward for effort is difficult when you don't see actual physical cash. By equating possessions, or lack of them, as signs of success, self-esteem may be tied to thinking certain goods, products and lifestyle trimmings are required in order to feel valued. The inability to obtain these prestigious items can result in the plummeting of a child's confidence and they may blame their parents.

Another custom that undermines children's confidence is equating success with participation rather than achievement. If they expect to be rewarded for every behaviour by word or deed, they're likely to be constantly seeking external approval for every one of their actions, no matter how insignificant.

Schools, recognising this issue, have introduced resilience programs. Rewarding only first, second and third-place getters enhances children's awareness that not everyone wins, and they are encouraged to strive for improvement. Parents, teachers and significant adults' explanations and support counters damaging self-doubt.

Lack of confidence about appearance can be found in even the youngest of children. Resilience is important in a world where stories of bullying among children abound. Together with adolescents and emerging adults, they need skills to withstand the pressure of equating appearance with being valued.

Minds and bodies change with age. From childhood through to the teenage years and beyond, siblings and peers pick up on each other's physical vulnerabilities. Almost innately, they seem to know what will most upset each other when it comes to appearance.

The most marked changes occur in puberty. At this time boys and girls become sexually mature. It follows a predictable pattern. However, each individual is different. As bodies change in shape, early maturing females may be especially vulnerable to lower self-esteem and poor body image.

Adults are under pressure too, especially if you've had a history of low self-esteem since childhood. As an adult, you may be mortified to notice signs that you're ageing. You'll remove concrete examples, such as lines, once described as signs of laughter and character from a life well-lived. You may have injections for fuller lips and plumped-out cheeks and other treatments, including lasering, to remove the normal signs of ageing.

Undervaluing the things that make you special and unique, makes you susceptible to propaganda advertisers' hype and peer pressure. If your confidence is on shaky ground, it's easy to diminish your inherent value and discard common sense. Instead, you buy products and/or engage in costly treatments and memberships knowing they yield little or no lasting result.

Surrendering your beliefs for the advertised ideals of a perfect face and body minimises or ignores your essence. The beauty industry offers a huge constantly changing suite of services to modify your appearance. From young girls to older males, none are omitted from their highly developed emotive strategies designed to pressure you into involvement with their beauty treatments.

Based on your observations of models and movie stars, notorious for focussing on appearance, do you emulate their messages about retaining your looks and remaining forever young? Do you think that all it takes is a simple treatment and you'll be transformed into the younger and/or more attractive version of yourself?

The list of service providers who feed your self-doubt is growing all the time. Treatments are offered for everyone from teenagers to adults. Rather than enhancing aspects of your natural beauty with makeup and fashionable clothing, you may even believe that you need surgical intervention.

Treatments

Treatments are no longer the reserve of Hollywood movie stars or other famous people. Nor are they limited to those with injuries or who show obvious deterioration through ageing. Mothers even take their daughters to sessions for pampering at younger and younger ages, creating the perception in the young person that appearance is important and engaging with the beauty industry for treatments is normal.

Facialists report that strong ingredients found in many of the products obtained by children aren't appropriate for their age group, but the strength of the imagery is addictive. Keen to follow trends without a thought for the consequences, they don't realise that products like retinol or Vitamin A, which stimulate skin cell turnover, may cause irritation, redness and sensitivity and damage healthy young skin.

Cosmetic Injectables

Cosmetic injectables have become commonplace, replacing the face-lift phenomenon. There are a huge variety of treatments and dozens of businesses willing to take your money. The cosmetic industry, a highly renumerated business model, is not regulated.

According to the Cosmetic Physicians College of Australasia (CPCA), in Australia, the cosmetic industry is estimated to be worth more than $1 billion[1]. Botox and other fillers in a non-medical setting may be applied by medical professionals looking to either supplement their current position or move into the world of aesthetics. Beauty enhancement treatments target all age groups.

Mothers told me of giving their daughters Botox or beauty salon vouchers 'just in case' to circumvent the possibility of developing frown or other facial lines forming in the future! In some countries, Botox is routinely available from dentists but Australian regulations usually preclude them from offering Botox. Today's cosmetic dentist provides far more than hygiene or restorative dentistry. Even do-it-yourself teeth-whitening kits are now commonplace.

Surgery

The demand for surgery continues to grow. Plastic surgeons offer implants for women, including breast augmentation, Brazilian butt lifts and/or other buttock procedures. But surgery is no longer the purvey of females alone. Males also have various implants including 'abs', as well as surgery on stomach, arms and/or noses in pursuit of the perfect body.

Liposuction and the demand for gastric stomach stapling and other forms of bariatric surgery for weight loss remains popular with males and females as do the more serious surgical enhancements such as butt lifts and tummy tucks. Males for whom gym workouts have not resulted in the desired abdominal muscular appearance or for whom the passing of age is made obvious as body parts droop, may also opt for surgical implants to create an appearance of well-defined muscular 'abs' or engage in body tattoos and piercings as well as skin treatments.

There are times when an operation or procedure goes wrong. One of my clients had a stomach stapling operation that resulted in him being incapacitated for life. He told me that his whole body went into meltdown as his organs overheated and literally melted. It was doubtful he would pull through. Although he did, he can never walk or manage an independent life anymore.

Reality television is compelling viewing for audiences but isn't real life despite the moniker. For a chilling vision of where these operations can lead in the search for beauty, there are television programs featuring some of the more bizarre results. *Botched* is one example of a reality TV show that reveals some of the unintended physical consequences of plastic surgery gone wrong[2].

Unlike the televised personalities exhorting surgical intervention, it's not your only choice. Allowing yourself to become fixated with media and popular personalities can inadvertently create potential problems for your well-being.

Gyms

Gyms and exercise classes are now a permanent fixture in our culture. Decades of fitness crazes have seen them flourish among children through to adults, along with the idea that changing yourself physically equates to greater confidence. Even children are susceptible to the smallest obsession about their flaws and want to do training. We see women wanting to know how to burn calories quickly turn to exercise classes. Men spend hours at gyms using weights and changing to high-protein diets to help them create the toned physique they like to show off in tight t-shirts.

The fact that gymnasiums are located in high-rise apartment blocks reinforces the message to exercise. So do specialist gyms for over 50s and workplaces incorporating gyms (or letting staff know about their nearest one if it's not located within the office building). The emphasis is on talking about maintaining a healthy appearance. Staff will vie for chances to outdo each other, even older males, when recounting their exercise routine.

Fashion

Throughout the ages, especially for the female shape, fashion has been transformed. The hourglass shape of actresses such as Marilyn Munroe was represented as ideal from the 1930s to the 1950s. Women with skinny, boyish body types developed in the 1920s were encouraged to take weight gain supplements to become more curvaceous.

The male image was of a clean-cut, athletic and lean man. The arrival of the Beatles saw an emphasis on men's hairstyles, embracing longer cuts, sideburns, ponytails or afros, made popular by the counterculture in the music industry.

The 1980s exhorted a tall, athletic-shaped woman with toned arms. The male ideal, popularised by icons such as Arnold Schwarzenegger, incorporated body building and huge, bulging muscles. The 1990s brought another change. This time it was a waif-like body shape, celebrated by model Kate Moss, which consisted of extreme thinness in an androgynous body. That fashion was dubbed heroin chic.

The rise of social media, together with augmentation procedures, has resulted in women today in the hourglass yet thin body shape. This entails a combination of enlarged breasts, lips and glutes in the buttock region in an otherwise very thin body. Men's ideal body shape is now a more achievable dad bod – a healthy but not too chiselled or defined shape, topped by a neat, tidy, easily-managed haircut.

Retailers use their knowledge of changing body shapes by catering with fashions for women outside the standard size 14 and males and females identifying as different genders. They increasingly seek out models of all shapes and sizes, realising that promoting fashion only in particular sizes is bad for business. Consequently, we now have plus-size models (size 18) alongside size 8 models.

Hair

Hair is an area of pride for many people so hair loss, whether through ageing or illness, can be a major hurdle. Conceit among men used to centre on hair loss. Fashions have changed with music idols shaving their heads, and even in parliamentary circles, we have a leader of a party with a shaved head. Rather than being bald, in situations with receding hairlines and actual hair loss, some males sport hairpieces, toupees or complete wigs, many of which are obvious.

Cancer treatments are known to cause hair loss and it can be an extra burden on an already unwell woman. The incidence of cancer has risen rapidly in the post-COVID-19 era, thus hairpieces and wigs provided by philanthropic organisations continue to offer a much-needed solution. For women who lost their hair following cancer treatments, it is one positive method to restoring a little confidence.

Have you noticed that even media personalities such as newsreaders, early morning breakfast announcers and other regular television personalities have the same hairstyle each day? Is this vanity or to make life easier, or both? It's possible because they too wear wigs for each broadcast.

Tattooists

Tattooists have burgeoned in popularity. It's now a career path and provides a lucrative business return. Removal of them is big business too. Many women have their eyebrows tattooed. Others have tattoos in a discreet place but some males and females have almost covered their entire bodies in ink. This incurs a huge expense.

Some hairdressers work from home but each major shopping centre has barbers and hair salons. In addition to at least one facility for beauty treatments, in many centres, additional beautification services including false nails, manicures, pedicures and/or false eyelashes are often available.

Tanning Studios

Tanning studios happily provide a service if you believe in the benefits of a tan as do many girls and women. When attending important functions they routinely turn to tanning studios or purchase home-based spray-on tans. After years of indoctrination about the dangers of the sun and being told that there is no such thing as a safe tan, these strategies negate the risks of skin cancer associated with over exposure to the sun's ultraviolet (UV) rays.

Children and adults alike have been taught about the dangers. We've been told that solariums, tanning beds, sunbeds and sunlamps, which were commonly used until more recent revelations, are associated with eye damage, premature skin ageing and an increased risk of developing skin cancer. Despite this, a lack of confidence can override common sense. The belief that a tan denotes good health continues. A large contingent can still be seen sunbaking on every public beach.

Making the most of the body you have been given is a new concept for many people. Imagine how it would feel not to worry. Think about the paradox of a beautiful blossom. Once achieving perfection, the blossom withers and dies. In nature, perfect beauty doesn't last. It's reborn.

Perfection and Comparisons

In a youth-obsessed, results-driven culture it can seem that as soon as we reach one of our goals the posts are moved away. In these circumstances, it's impossible to achieve an idealised self no matter how many beauty treatments, days at the gym or substances purchased in the name of health you have.

If perfection is your goal there's always something else to change. Irrespective of what you do to improve your health or how much work you put into your relationships, careers or academic achievements, there is always something or someone better, younger, fitter, healthier and more successful.

The attempt to achieve perfection can be remorseless. It drains your energy, takes valuable time from family, friends and self-care, and gets in the way of relaxation. As soon as you reach an 'ideal' shape, look, fashion or level of achievement, the message changes.

If we carry on emphasising appearance at this rate who knows where it will end? We already have deaths linked to bullying about appearance, weight and body shape. We seem to have forgotten how to enjoy what we have, not settling for inner beauty or the bodies we've been given.

Self-doubt is not reserved for a particular gender, culture, race or age group. We're all susceptible to societal pressure. Over the years, clients, friends, family members, colleagues and acquaintances have all revealed similar fears. They worried about ageing, failing at school or in the tertiary environment, weight gain or loss, relationships, being replaced at work and feeling too old to get another job. They complained about never following their passions, feeling unwanted, being lonely and feeling trapped in a body beginning to break down through ageing. They feared not being skilled enough, attractive enough, smart enough, a good enough parent, wealthy enough, physically strong enough, healthy enough, shapely enough, thin enough or young enough!

Reinforced by the media, peers, family or friends, have you developed the discomforting and painful habit of constantly comparing yourself with others? If your confidence was shaky for whatever reason, but particularly in relation to career, relationships and/or ageing, the emphasis on maintaining a certain youthful appearance at every age can seriously impact your well-being.

Judging yourself and others is a recipe for a merry-go-round of discontent. Constantly making comparisons, trying to look the same regardless of your differences in age or physical characteristics, berating yourself for your imperfections, seeking equivalent looks and status notwithstanding your skills and abilities, is a recipe for disappointment. It will severely impact your confidence.

Rather than comparing yourself with others as a means of feeling better, enhance aspects of your natural beauty. For example, use makeup, alter your hairstyle, and dress in fashionable clothing. Instead of feeling anxious because you think you must look perfect or that the only thing you can control is the way you look, you can embrace what you've been given!

Choices and Helpful Thinking

Trying to mimic the behaviour of famous people is unrealistic and only reinforces negative thinking. Even the most well-known people have gone to extraordinary lengths in their pursuit of beauty or to deal with their unhappiness. Despite looking beautiful and being feted wherever she went, the late Diana,

Princess of Wales was known to be unhappy. She dealt with her unhappiness by focussing on food, starving herself, or excessive over-eating then purging, resulting in an eating disorder. This was her unhealthy method for dealing with stressful thoughts about her marriage.

Instead of feeling helpless, greater awareness of the way thoughts contribute to feelings and behaviours can result in a more favourable outcome. It's easy to yield to negative self-talk about your body shape and size and/ or your achievements when that same old tape playing in your head is 'you are not good enough/ you are too fat/too thin/you are unhealthy/you are not fit enough/you are too old'.

Which aspects of your thinking and behaviour impact positively or otherwise on your well-being? Does it result from your earliest memories of what people told you?

Do you still feel the impact of being bullied at school, at university, by family members or in a workplace about some feature of your appearance, your physical skills, academic ability or when you expressed a certain point of view?

Young people have always been subjected to schoolyard bullying. Even before early primary school years, being excluded from social events destroyed confidence. Nevertheless, regardless of your earlier experiences, it's how you think about them that governs your responses.

You absorbed, both consciously and subliminally, the messages portrayed in the family, in your social circles, in the media and by your peers. But because you have been given free will, you also have the power to choose.

Constantly comparing yourself or trying to match someone else's expectations does nothing for your self-confidence. Making comparisons between yourself and others who you presume are younger, more talented, beautiful or attractive will always leave you feeling dissatisfied as no two people are the same.

Don't beat yourself up if you fall into unhelpful self-talk. Try to let go of any self-limiting beliefs and behaviours associated with unhelpful thinking instead of making unfavourable comparisons or taking someone else's word about your appearance. It says more about them than you. After all, if they were truly confident, they wouldn't need to try and put you down. It is their issue, not yours.

Attempting to match someone else by reaching similar goals, however outrageous, may create compelling viewing for television and YouTube audiences, but it's not real life. We can't all engage in seismic activities that change the world.

Do you really want to have a television camera follow your every move as you make the changes, or sit in your room talking to a video camera while broadcasting your face to the world? Many children and young people are quite happy to do it, but are you?

What you look like, how many qualifications, careers, houses, shoes or other possessions you have accumulated will be meaningless in the afterlife. While you're here, you can manage your reactions to what people say.

By thinking differently, you'll only take on board things that are helpful. Avoid the rest. It's irrelevant. Build your confidence by accepting your genetics. Work on what you want to change or not. The choices you make need to suit your beliefs and way of life.

Don't give in to something that doesn't fit your lifestyle or values because of exposure to media, education campaigns or advice from health professionals. When you feel pressured by individuals, businesses or corporations, check in to see if you're allowing them to steal your confidence.

Confident thinking enables you to alter your priorities but even the best of plans can go awry. You can have all the comforts that money can buy, the most prestigious career, the most buffed and toned body, the most noteworthy friends and minimal outward signs of ageing, but a diagnosed medical condition or life-changing event can arise out of the blue and alter your whole life in an instant.

Things are *not* set in stone. Once you learn to dispute many of your negative responses, including worries about growing older, you can replace your faulty thinking with a kinder and more realistic view of yourself. Health issues can then be viewed as just another step along the path that is your life's journey.

As you recognise and decode any unhelpful thought processes, you can examine them to find who put these ideas in your head. Once you know where they came from, you can decide if you still hold the same beliefs about these issues. Are they consistent with your values? Do they fit your current life stage and circumstances?

Once you're aware of how your thinking has impacted on your life, you can find the confidence to turn your thinking around. Choose to be a self-assured adult, happy with your appearance, knowing that there is someone to whom you look beautiful and they're not worried about your age, weight, fitness, health or appearance.

Being confident and insightful enables you to model positivity. It's helpful in influencing others, including the younger generation.

Sharing your insights can help them avoid the pitfalls of blindly following advertisements made by big businesses and the weight loss or cosmetic industries. You can model conscious changes to your faulty thinking as a means of managing a predisposition to low self-esteem.

The Characteristics of Confident People

In conversations, research and my work with confident women and men, I found that they share similar characteristics.

Integrity

Firstly, they exhibit a strong sense of integrity. Several of the people with whom I spoke quoted, as if from the singer Billy Joe Royal album with the same title, that they respectfully 'tell it like it is', referring to the fact that they are open and honest with other people. For example, they don't misrepresent themselves in interviews.

When forming relationships or creating an online profile for dating or work, they're devoid of artifice. They're open about their appearance and reveal their situations and life circumstances honestly. They don't hide behind the achievements of others or take credit for something they didn't do.

Confident folk accept blame when it is warranted but they won't espouse views they disagree with just for the sake of being popular with a certain group. Nor do they adopt political correctness or what we now refer to as 'woke' behaviour. They think for themselves, analyse situations and events and hold views consistent with their own values. Their actions in business and life are honourable.

Courage

Secondly, confident people show courage. This doesn't mean they act hastily or dangerously. Certain risky occupations are associated with bravery. For example, farmers regularly require a strong nerve to deal with adversity arising from the loss of their animals in droughts or floods. Community-minded, brave farmers in many countries united because food production and their livelihoods were threatened by government edicts over their farmlands.

Many emergency and helping professionals also demonstrate courage and stamina when dealing with difficult, often life-threatening situations. An item in a Melbourne paper, the *Herald Sun*, in August 2023, illustrated their trials, quoting that 'Up to 40 emergency workers are allegedly being attacked every week as the police union warns assailants targeting officers are using a loophole.'[3] These confident people are models of resilience, demonstrating support for those less fortunate than themselves. Yet the same people don't feel the need to self-aggrandise.

Energy

Thirdly, confident people exude energy. They get things done. Hence the expression, reputedly made by statesman Benjamin Franklin or attributed to comedian Lucille Ball, 'If you want something done, give it to a busy person.' It's pleasing to be in the company of people who direct positive energy to the task at hand. It's different from being too busy. Those people have a habit of burying themselves in work, a behaviour they've adopted as an avoidance strategy. Their busy-ness is likely to be a cover for anxiety.

Truly energetic, outgoing, optimistic people are attractive. Their energy disperses to those around them. You are probably joyful and light-hearted when in their company.

Self-awareness

Fourthly self-awareness is a strength of confident people. They appraise themselves realistically, without resorting to self-deprecation or false modesty when describing their appearance. They acknowledge their age if required and honestly reflect on their accomplishments but don't dwell on them to the detriment of others. They accept praise when it's warranted. They admit their strengths and weaknesses without judgement and concede that they have areas for improvement.

Good Philosophy

The Confidage philosophy entices you to pay attention to and thereby enhance your confidence. Embracing this as your philosophy directs you to consciously think about issues such as the pressures to alter your appearance, but it's also about negotiating life's changes, especially as you age, and speaking about and managing the challenges when dealing with a world that's constantly changing.

Congratulations on your efforts to negotiate and manage everything while the planet, governments, the economy, the environment, your relationships, values, goals, interactions between countries and technology change society more rapidly than for any previous generations.

The word Confidage is a term created to help you focus on accepting everything about yourself unconditionally. Thinking in these terms is a reminder to deal with and manage change realistically whilst maintaining optimism regardless of your body's physical changes or your emotional responses to your looks, cognitive and physical abilities, age or health. Thus, theoretically, Confidage directs your thinking towards greater self-assurance about ageing with the outcome being enhanced confidence.

Living in a global environment where the pace of change is rapid requires constant adaptation. Youth adapt more quickly. A younger generation may look to their elders for wisdom and offer support, whereas being more technologically savvy, they help older generations navigate the changes wrought by living in an AI and technology-driven era.

Many bosses today are younger than their staff, thus older workers can lose confidence. If you're from an older cohort, you may notice your insecurity or the same among your peers if a new manager replaces an older worker. You may have personally experienced anxiety when working with a new manager or colleague young enough to be your child.

Additionally, if you're confronted by a relationship breakdown because of divorce or death, it exacerbates your anxiety. The fear of being unwanted and alone, coupled with getting older, can result in dread and things that previously seemed insignificant assume more importance. It's therefore unsurprising that this results in people taking steps to counter the signs of natural ageing.

Today's lifestyle and working expectations are vastly different from bygone eras. Previous generations had little time for the insecurities besieging our modern 21st-century globalised society. The fortitude of pioneers and early settlers was necessary for survival. Working in a harsh landscape to develop the land turned skins lined and leathery. Confronted with the need for basic survival, few had the time or relative affluence to indulge in beauty treatments. As they were active every day growing food, tending to animals and working for something as simple as obtaining clean water, they didn't need exercise classes. Always busy, untouched by fashion or trends, they aged confidently. There was no time for vanity. They were confident of support from each other. Our modern prosperous nation, a country with abundant food, energy and resources, has come about thanks to their energy and hard work.

Lacking their serenity and with more time to reflect on image, in today's Western world we engage in treatments and fashions designed to change aspects of our bodies. It's concerning that even deaths have been linked to bullying about appearance, weight, body shape, loss of confidence and shattered self-esteem.

Maybe you shrug off compliments because you don't think you're attractive. You may denigrate your achievements in the workplace. You can spend a great deal of effort being busy when you're attempting to stave off anxiety about being replaced by a younger or smarter person in the workplace or relationships. If you can tap into your inner confidence, appearance and age won't matter.

Child or adult, imagine how liberating it would be if, rather than fighting the ageing process or continuously comparing yourself to others, you simply acknowledged yourself and your situation in life without making any changes. Rescue yourself philosophically and metaphorically with the knowledge that you don't have to conform to a particular behaviour, look or style, no matter who sets the agenda, from fashion houses to peers. You don't have to accept the vision others have for you! Don't let anyone else control or direct you to subscribe to their particular goals as if it's the only way to live a rewarding life.

Living Longer

People worldwide are living longer. Today, for the first time in history, most people can expect to live well beyond their sixties. The pace of population ageing around the world is increasing dramatically. However, reviewing healthy ageing processes and research about the normal ageing process reveals it's not the same for everyone[4].

Nor is it the same in every country. Demographics vary between countries but ageing is a factor for all. Japan is one of the world's fastest-ageing societies with a record 36.25 million people aged over 65 according to a newspaper report[5].

Today, 125 million people are aged 80 years or older. By 2050, the world's population aged 60 years and older is expected to total 2 billion, up from 900 million in 2015. There will be almost this many (120 million) living in China alone, and 434 million people in this age group worldwide. By then, 80% of all older people will live in low and middle-income countries.

Interestingly, there's little evidence to suggest that older people today are experiencing better health in their later years than their parents. While rates of severe disability have declined in high-income countries over the past 30 years, there has been no significant change in mild to moderate disability over the same period.

This has implications for planners but is so much easier for you individually if you have an inner confidence. You can freely acknowledge any physical frailties realistically and enjoy others unconditionally. Being more aware of and tolerant of differences, especially related to your physical body, mind, behaviours and imperfections exacerbated with age, brings greater peace.

Wherever you live, if you can experience these extra years of life in good health and live in a supportive environment, your ability to do the things you value will be little different from that of a younger person. A longer life brings with it opportunities to pursue new activities such as further education, a new career or pursuing a long-neglected passion such as playing an instrument. If you're an older person, you can contribute in many ways to families and communities. Being involved with others impacts your adaptation to healthy ageing and psychosocial growth, although it's dependent on your interests and health.

Some people age early, whereas others are not frail even into their 90s. How you age is associated with many physical and emotional factors. It depends on how you approach change, particularly at points of transition, including those related to work or geographical relocation. Your circumstances are unique. Your circumstances may be comparable with others, but nothing is exactly the same for any two people.

It's important to reflect on your life favourably, guided by your inner confidence. It strengthens your ability to withstand negative self-judgements and pressure from external forces at any age, especially as it's inevitable that you will change because we all grow older.

The changes aren't linear. They're only loosely associated with chronological age. Awareness of the impact on your life associated with your biological parents, your sex and ethnicity improves your mastery of age.

There are natural downsides to growing older that cannot be avoided, despite the beauty industry's exhortations. By the time you were in your 30s, your cells began to die off, and even unseen, your body began to change. Your brain mass has altered. No matter how many varieties of workouts you do, the latest fad food or diet modifications you have, your brain and body lose some zing as you age. But not everyone's development is the same.

In your 30s you could question what kind of person you were as young adulthood ended. Friendships, some dating back to school days, were well-established. Your self-esteem had developed. You might have thought you had to present an image consistent with remaining forever young.

In your 40s, changes to your body exposed the first early signs of mortality. However, with confidence, you can/have thrive(d) in your 40s, 50s and beyond. Ageing is more than a biological process. It's cultural, cerebral, spiritual and emotional. Cultural mores have a profound effect on confidence. It may impact matters as diverse as clothing through to physical image.

Resilience in the face of adversity and obvious enjoyment when participating in an active lifestyle isn't bound to any age category. Health factors are not confined to a particular age group either, although some aspects may be genetic.

Eating a balanced diet, refraining from consuming excess alcohol and not smoking, when combined with physical activity and strength training exercises goes a long way to helping combat any loss of physical capacity. These things help you mentally too.

Sure, ageing increases the risk of biological problems. Your cells age and exposure to too much sun in your earlier years shows up in damage to your skin. You may also be prescribed glasses due to changes in your eyesight over the years. As yet, we don't have a full picture of changes to eyesight due to the increased exposure to iPhones and other technology.

How you age is associated with many factors, including life transitions, relocation, death of a partner or a health issue. Your lifestyle, physical and social environment, together with your personal traits are important factors in determining your physical and emotional well-being at any age.

Even when you're at the pinnacle of success and seem to have things running smoothly, an event can arise out of the blue that alters your whole life in an instant. However, thinking confidently can ameliorate many of the losses and enhance your adaptation to new situations.

Happiness isn't dependent on achieving or maintaining a certain appearance or having particular life roles, relationships and achievements by a certain age regardless of circumstances. Contentment and confidence aren't dependent on age or life stage.

You will be unhappy if you constantly focus on seeing others as younger, more beautiful or more attractive. The challenge is to recognise if fear of standing out from the crowd, fear of being different, fear of rejection, of being judged, of feeling less than perfect as you age is behind that unhappiness.

When the airwaves are filled with propaganda about an idealised image of what you *should* look like, it's easy to lose sight of reality. There are definitely some changes to your body due to age, but the differences are connected to physical characteristics, your environment, what family you were born into, health and your genetic history.

Maybe you reject or minimise your individual needs and your environment to focus on pleasing everyone else and/or negate the realities of your life stage. You may be fearful about being seen as less than competent, especially as you grow older.

It takes inordinate energy to defend or deny where you are in terms of your current life stage or your physical and mental health. Victims of self-doubt can have all the outward trappings of success and every comfort that money can buy but it doesn't fill the confidence void. Developing a toned body, fraternising with the most noteworthy people and showing little outward signs of ageing may be just a way of hiding unhappiness and insecurity.

On the other hand, confidence enables you to recognise that success and acceptance aren't achieved because you maintain an eternally youthful appearance. You understand that as appearances differ, what is attractive to one person is not the same for everyone else. Thus, you don't need to make any changes in order to feel valued. You enjoy yourself and others unconditionally, regardless of any imperfections in looks or worrying about what to say.

If some days it all feels too much, and your energy has deserted you, don't worry. We all have good days and not so good days, when our confidence is lowered for a multitude of reasons. At those times is important to remember the little things in your life that are the most important. Those special moments you may not even put into words that made you feel important. Don't put off things until you have time, or delay doing things until you are utterly confident of the outcome. Remember good times, look forward to a bright future and breathe it all in.

Chapter Three

Maintaining healthy behaviours throughout life improves physical capacity, which is especially important as the years pass. It's also important that you don't neglect cognitive activities. There are ways to preserve your physical and mental capacity.

It's natural to exercise when young, even for most children enamoured with technology, by engaging in organised sports or remember the good times as you look forward to a bright future playing with pets, siblings and friends. However, as we mature, life gets in the way. Physical exercise can be the last thing on your mind, whereas you can stay sharp cognitively through fun activities including social interactions, brain puzzles such as sudoku, learning a new language, being involved in cultural or musical activities and travel.

Exercise for Your Age

Peers and health professionals are quick to advocate beauty and fitness regimes for optimum functioning. They espouse the importance of exercise and healthy eating, but once your body responds to ageing, it takes more effort to maintain strength and health. The fitness you took for granted in your youth requires more effort as you get older. You could be among the many who find every excuse not to exercise and then become caught up in the cycle of self-blame.

Don't be deterred if this applies to you. Maybe you need to find new, different and/or appropriate exercises and activities that fit your lifestyle. If you combine exercise with socialisation, you've metaphorically killed two birds with one stone as both contribute to your well-being.

Strength training helps maintain muscle mass, and good nutritional behaviour plus a positive mind-set helps preserve your mental faculties. Even if you're confident about your appearance, physical health and social life, it's nevertheless equally important to focus on your mental health. It helps you continue if you enjoy and feel proud of your exercise routine.

If organised exercise is not for you, but you're busy with housework, you're already physically active. Marriage and child-rearing combined with full-time or even part-time work often puts paid to any time for formal exercise. Parents of young children (or the grandparents who help out), already busy running around, taking children here and there for sport and musical or other group activities after school, are time-poor. At least the act of being so physically busy somewhat negates the need for formal exercise.

If you're a new mum, maybe you've joined a Mum and Bubs group. Meeting as a group with your children in strollers, it's enjoyable to combine walking as you talk with others who have similar issues. Conversing with other parents at school pick-up also enhances confidence as you have a shared understanding of situations and the environment. Alternatively, you may join a school support on-line group as a means of being informed about activities related to the children's school life or decide to have a group weekend away at a spot where there are plenty of things to keep everyone active.

Getting together with family and friends affords an opportunity to combine leisure with exercise – perhaps walking to a barbecue at the beach, engaging in family cricket matches or making time for more organised sporting activities. Once you put your mind to it, the list is endless.

Men and some women get together for cycling on weekends in small groups or extend their get-togethers from fitness to social activities. Weekend events that incorporate health, fun and fitness also include bush walking, beach activities, volunteering support at surf or other sporting clubs and meet-ups with participants who share similar goals. Being active together doesn't require a focus on the individual and that may help you relax.

Work and other commitments can be time-consuming. If you lack the time, interest, energy or opportunity to exercise, you can become caught up in the unhelpful cycle of self-blame. As well as responding to age, when you make lifestyle changes, it requires more effort to consciously engage in exercise. If you prefer, simply get outdoors and take a stroll to interact with nature. Talk with the neighbours about the environment.

Workplaces also realise the benefits of healthy staff. There are team-building days that often involve fun-filled activities that use energy too, such as line dancing or salsa classes. Individuals often plan regular walks with colleagues after work and/or gym sessions in the evening or before work.

Depending on your life stage, goals and circumstances, you may even be involved in unexpected events such as an accident or health issue that impacts your exercise and/or appearance. When your priorities alter, it's how you manage your circumstances that impacts how you cope. It's largely dependent on your attitude.

Sometimes we exercise to enhance our confidence. This may result in over-exercising rather than enjoying it as a social and fun activity. Family members can have a profound influence on your confidence and habits can develop because of jealousy.

For example, my mother was teased in childhood by her stick-thin sister. Photos show my mother engaged in multiple sports. Dogged by her sister's taunts that she was uncoordinated and chubby, my mother developed the habit of telling herself that if she ate certain portions or 'bad' foods she must punish herself with exercise.

Subliminal messages can be carried throughout life with little awareness of how the idea formed and result in negative feelings around food and exercise. By telling herself that certain foods were 'bad remember the good times as you look forward to a bright future' and that exercise was 'good', my mother risked feeling 'bad' if she ate sweets or was too busy to exercise.

It took years before she could indulge her sweet tooth and enjoy being one of the team in sports. Finally, in adulthood, she relaxed. She began to enjoy the social aspect of sports, including tennis and golf, and by growing her own food she always had a healthy, balanced diet so food was no longer an issue. She was always fit, as she loved to garden even in her nineties and she lived a long, healthy life. Conversely, her sister was high maintenance, became unwell, and died at an early age.

Have you been jealous of family members or others who seem to eat what they like, not do much in the way of exercise, yet seem so confident, strong and healthy-looking?

Try journalling as you ask yourself the following questions:

- Are they really confident or covering up their lack of self-esteem by showing off or covering a personality defect?
- Is their outward manifestation of self-assurance based on telling us how

prestigious their school or university was, boasting about their significant career or arrogantly citing their association with important, influential or successful people?

- Are they hung up on who they know and the occupations of their parents or children, the size of their house, the make of their car, where to go for holidays, whether or not they have wealthy friends, and the size of their bank balance as well as age and physique?

Take a moment to reflect on what you have written. Where did your thoughts take you as you contemplated these questions? There are no right or wrong answers and no one will judge your responses. You are a detective – uncovering aspects of your own life and the journey that brought you into being who you are today.

Habits and bodily changes exacerbate with age. So what? Take charge of making your habits positive. If you're blessed with inner confidence, you exude energy. You habitually give and receive acceptance regardless of age or stage of life. You know that all the comforts that money can buy and outward physical perfection don't equal contentment if you have a dearth of confidence.

In our society, ageing is equated with the (absurd) idea that older people are a burden and have nothing to contribute. Despite the cultural obsession with maintaining a youthful appearance, if you're confident you won't be preoccupied with exercising in order to slow down and/or adjust to ageing.

Reaching maturity is an opportunity for self-reflection. On the other hand, if you lack self-esteem, you and/or others may regard the physical or cognitive signs of ageing with distaste. Such thinking may lead to insecurity, as Lynnette discovered.

Lynette – Ageism in the Workplace

Lynette's story is not unusual. The starting point in her narrative was the day her new manager called her into his office. Initially surprised, she had little forewarning of how that meeting was to change her life.

It transpired that the purpose of the meeting was to inform her that her job had been reclassified, therefore she was redundant. The news was devastating. In one fell swoop, she learnt she was no longer employed.

What hurt her the most was learning that in the restructure her role had been subsumed into a new position occupied by someone she'd mentored. Not only had Lynette been particularly attached to that girl, she'd formed a special bond with her because she represented the daughter Lynette never had. Lynette was shocked that she'd put so many years into the role as a loyal employee, going over and above what was expected, only to be replaced by someone so much younger.

Finally, her natural coping style kicked in and she talked out the ageing issue with family and friends. Lynette's former colleagues kept in contact with her socially. Through them, she learnt that the manager had a history of surrounding himself with younger people so they weren't surprised. However, aware that this practice was not uncommon, the older employees were fearful.

Talking over her situation with friends, Lynette found many of them, like her former work colleagues, were also caught up in a vicious cycle of fear about ageing. Older friends were overwhelmed with worry about being replaced by someone younger at work and/or in their personal relationships.

Having these conversations, Lynette recognised the rationale behind a phenomenon she'd previously failed to notice among friends her own age. It explained why so many rushed out to spend money on the latest clothing, beauty product or treatment, fads they'd spruiked to Lynette but which she'd politely declined.

Lynette didn't suffer from anxiety but was concerned for one friend in particular, which was the purpose of her visit. The more she talked about it, the more Lynette became aware of her friend's fear. She'd described feeling that her only control was over her physical being. Lynette believed her friend's lost confidence resulted from wanting to be the same as the glamorous and well-known figures she followed on social media.

She'd reacted to social media 'influencers', as well as media 'personalities', movie stars, musicians, politicians. Clever advertising, especially targeting females, definitely worked on Lynette's friend. Feeling pressured, she'd already submitted to expensive treatments.

She was trapped in a cycle of discontent. She constantly berated herself to Lynette about any perceived or real imperfections. Seeking equivalent looks and irrespective of reality left her seriously despondent.

On the other hand, Lynette had always remained resistant to suggestions that she undergo any treatments. She'd been quite happy to dress well, look after her hair and use makeup to make the most of her features. Despite her friend's insistence that undergoing treatments to counter the signs of natural ageing would have resulted in not being replaced at work, she was doubtful. For Lynette, it no longer mattered and she tried to impart this rationale to her friend. She was comfortable with being true to her age.

She was not out of work long. People from her network, knowing her skills and discovering she was available on the job market once more, spread the word. Soon she had a job offer with even better pay.

That restructure had other positive consequences too. Lynette's new position was closer to home. This meant less time commuting. Soon she was surrounded by a new group with whom she felt equally comfortable.

Lynette had her life back on track but continued to worry about her friend, who had bought into the whole injectables ideology but was oblivious to the fact that it did nothing for her anxiety. Lynette tried to show her that it was pointless to worry about younger people taking her job but she'd run out of strategies.

Lynette's self-confidence had returned but she realised that her friend was not as resilient. Through our work, Lynette agreed she could do no more. She decided to suggest to her friend that she seek a referral for her own professional help to come to terms with the fact that there would continue to be many bosses who are younger than their employees, especially in this technological era.

The Younger Boss

As well as worry about physical appearance, the requirement to keep up with the latest developments in technology presents another hurdle for some older workers. A younger boss makes them feel uncomfortable. They find themselves losing confidence in the workplace. This is especially noticeable among those in Lynette's generation. They were born just after the Baby Boomer generation (circa 1946–1964).

Generational points are not an exact science but demographers and social analysts label the generations with similar approximations. They refer to those born between 1965 and 1979 as Generation X, from 1980 to 1994 as Millenials, from 1995 to 2009 as Generation Z, from 2101 to 2024 as Generation Alpha, and those born between 2025 and 2039 as Generation Beta[6].

These age groups include young males and females who like to make radical changes to their hair colour, tattoo themselves and join gyms. Baby boomers may make similar adjustments to stave off anxiety about an ageing appearance. Following the flush of youth, many contemporary adult men and women in business, offices, public service, education, health and other professional roles undertake cosmetic changes.

You may have noticed friends spending more time at the hair salon, stepping up gym sessions, running marathons, or spending time endlessly in the pursuit of the next diet in an attempt to stave off their anxiety about being replaced, like Lynette, by a younger person at work or in a relationship. Rather than embrace the experiences and insights of older people, in our culture, many believe that to retain your relationships and/or job requires constant effort to look younger than your chronological age.

No wonder people are beset by worries about not being pretty, fit, smart or young enough. However, as Lynette found, your age doesn't have to impede respect. You are as beautiful as you feel, notwithstanding external factors. Being a good friend, parent or sibling has no age limit. It's important to confront life head-on, as Lynette did, ready to move on to the next adventure. You won't find contentment if you stay locked up metaphorically or literally in your home.

Constant Adaptation to Changing Environments

Rapid Changes

The normal process of getting older, combined with societal and other changes related to rapidly developing technologies, can exacerbate dread and contribute to a loss of confidence.

Everywhere you turn, whether man-made or in response to nature, change is evident. It can be instantaneous. So rapid is the pace of change that sometimes you feel lost in the struggle to keep up with the complexities of life and the multitude of rules and regulations in contemporary society. Little wonder you seek ways to regain a sense of control.

From having to manage academic requirements as a student and then prove yourself competent in the workforce as an employee, many stressors impact self-esteem and confidence. On top of that, there's the challenge of the modern world to master up-to-date technology. This necessitates constantly checking your smartphone or other device, responding to instant messages, downloading information and responding to blogs and emails from work colleagues, businesses, peers, family, friends and other groups to which you belong.

No Longer Important

You need inner self-confidence to keep abreast of the changes, especially if you're in an older demographic positioned among impatient or derogatory younger people in the workplace. A complaint among older people is that, once they reach 50 years, they become invisible.

Regrettably, instead of embracing the wisdom of older generations in our culture, a youthful work generation often denigrates the attempts of elders who are trying to keep up. They may even avoid them altogether, thereby missing out on the wisdom inherent to experience. Focussing on someone else's vulnerability may be a way of avoiding their own insecurity.

You may be filled with self-doubt that leaves you worrying that you're unimportant. Age notwithstanding, everyone is vulnerable to insecurity. Maybe you believe the hype that happiness is associated with being young 'at heart', if not in years.

At different phases of life or after particularly high-impact events, such as coping with loneliness after tragedy, death, the disability of a loved one, personal illness or financial disaster life changes. But work or relationships with partners and significant others can break down at any stage.

Whilst the sudden death of a loved one can happen at any age, when you're alone, things that previously seemed unimportant take on new value. As the years pass, many factors induce loneliness. If you're lonely, you're particularly vulnerable. Add to this a lack of confidence, and common sense often flies out the window. Looking to bolster your confidence after a sad or difficult event, it may be a welcome distraction to give in to advertised product offers.

Scams

Yearning to remain valued by colleagues, friends and family, as well as to a special companion, you may seek reassurance about the way you look. A lack of confidence and a desperation to feel that you're still important can make you vulnerable to online scams. Who doesn't lack confidence about something, especially as the years pass?

People who have ulterior motives prey on the vulnerable, especially the single or elderly, but being swindled financially can happen at any age. We all need to be aware of con artists but if you're older and/or single you need to be especially vigilant as scammers have had the most success with that group because they know the signs of certain vulnerabilities.

Dating fraud worldwide is one of the more common rip-offs, such as Catfishing, a cruel and embarrassing trick. You could even be scammed into thinking you're buying an expensive product without viewing it in person or getting an invoice for something you haven't bought. Stop and think before sending money. Many millions of dollars are lost annually.

Don't be discouraged. Even the most outwardly confident people who want to change something about their looks can be the victim of fraudsters. We're susceptible to self-denigration about so many issues, any one of which can undermine your confidence regardless of where you are in your lifespan.

The cosmetic, health and fitness industries, aware of this, offer inducements cleverly designed to tempt you. Other nefarious scammers also take advantage of your propensity to make purchases online to manage your low mood or self-doubt. Buying products online may give you a temporary high as your endorphins or feel-good chemicals are released. Even if you wouldn't otherwise consider parting with money online, you can be so despondent that you may be seduced. But it doesn't last.

Positive Energy

It's human nature to want to feel important and belong. This may cause you to undertake an action or express a particular view just to fit in with the crowd. Likened to a herd mentality, it's most apparent among teenagers. For them, peer pressure is omnipotent. However, as an adult, you may have followed the crowd even when you disapproved of their direction. It takes great courage to walk alone because of adherence to your principles if this places you out of step with the majority.

This is when applying Confidage thinking can help you stay on track. How you think elicits energy so pulling your focus back to being confident can help you avoid losing positivity. Thinking positively is a major step forward.

Be encouraged as you realistically review your place in the world. It's important to consider your life roles and circumstances, your views of yourself, the influences that may or may not have remained with you and your observations about significant others.

Today's children and adults who are confident don't blindly accept the vision others have for them. Like them and your forefathers, practice living with a positive mindset. No matter what anyone else says or does, if you believe in yourself, that's enough! Just being yourself without any preconceived ideas of how you should act, say or what you should look like is enough to elicit positive energy.

You have the power to make every day count at any and every age. As you reflect on your journey and where you derive your energy from, consider the following:

1. Is the fear of standing out from the crowd, fear of being different, fear of rejection, of being judged, taking most of your energy?

2. Have you rejected or minimalised your individual needs to focus on everyone else, ignoring your environment, loss of energy and the impact on your confidence?

3. Do you spend too much energy defending, denying or trying to slow down ageing because you're scared of being seen as less than competent as you grow older?

If you recognise these as attacks on your self-esteem, you've passed a major hurdle. Congratulations on recognising the facts and facing your fears.

Let go of negative energy metaphorically or literally as you build your confidence. Accept your genetics and the effects of the environment you live(d) in. If you genuinely want to take steps to become mentally or emotionally fitter, change your eating habits, clothing and hairstyle, or even your glasses. Don't let anything or anyone stop you. Go ahead confidently. If you're tempted to turn to surgery, that's fine too but remember it only changes the surface and even the stars' magazine images are airbrushed.

As you think about your concerns, take a moment to think about the impact of your social world, society, culture, career, family and leisure pursuits. Is it time to broaden your interests, expand your friendship networks and meet with more positive, new, like-minded individuals and groups?

Chapter Four

No matter your chronological age, we live in unparalleled times. Since factories using coal began to modernise Europe, the world has progressed through many stages. Our lives evolve. From candles, we evolved to using electric lighting, from coal, we progressed to nuclear energy, then automation and robotics took over the work in factories and now we're amidst an era of rapid technological expansion.

Digital communications and the internet connect us worldwide. We're becoming more cognizant of the use of AI and technology, which invades every aspect of our lives. It can motivate or threaten your coping strategies as you try to survive modern life and changes to the basics, including parenting and education. It's not just in the workplace that you have to master new, unprecedented skills. The same is necessary in everyday life.

Today, irrespective of how many robotic inventions and interventions are created or how much the government, media and business impact our lives, some things are relatively unchanged. As humans, we maintain the same basic body structure, our psyche still flourishes with human contact and we all long to be appreciated.

When you're hugged, you experience warmth emanating from physically connecting with another person as well as feeling intrinsically valued. Knowing you are loved and needed for who you are, you don't worry about how you fit in, how you look or what you say to family members, friends or in wider society. As yet, neither technology nor external systems can fulfil, control or replace our basic desire to be cared for by another living creature.

Growing Up in a Cyber-World

Remember the joy and how heartwarming it is to see tiny children, so small they reach only the lower leg height of the adults, rush up to their parent figure and hug them around the legs as they're released from class after school? But have you also observed even the littlest preschooler being disinterested in their mother's hugs because s/he's been captured by technology? Or the child who, on greeting his mother as she asks about his day at school, looks down at his wristwatch to reply, 'I did 600 steps'?

In this technological era, as manufacturers present products that are alluring and easy to use, beginning in infancy, we hardly stop to think about what could be happening to these young minds gripped by technology.

Although intrusive, it can be helpful. Parents provide their children access to various forms of technology for educational and entertainment purposes. Technology used as a communication tool keeps parents and children connected.

Educators instruct us on using technology and communicate with parents about their children. Learning activities are provided using media and schoolwork is done using a computer screen in class before being continued at home. Schools also advertise events and promote other important matters to parents and share pictures from sporting festivities and other outings.

Twenty-first Century Challenges

Teachers face vastly different challenges emanating from children's ability to connect with all manner of groups and individuals. For example, teachers have to be 'in-serviced' about appropriately responding to and providing for children identifying as cats or inanimate objects. This is no longer an unusual phenomenon in the school environment as a secondary school principal explained to me and has been written about by others[7].

Self-worth is tied to your thinking. Children and teenagers mimic what they see at home, in school and online. Computer games may be associated with an increase in violence in the community. Even supposedly harmless computer games for children, such as one involving a chef chasing mice away from food, is a violent game as it necessitates a player (the chef), to throw knives and 'kill' the mice.

As online violence increases, relationship assaults increase. Easy access to online pornography changes the way young men think about women. Some young men today, modelling what they see online, think it's acceptable to behave roughly and violently towards women. Anecdotally, doctors, dealing with the resultant physical damage to a young person, have linked violent pornographic imagery to the harmful behaviours perpetrated on females. These young men may need help to build their self-esteem.

Cyber-safety

The speed and intensity of changes associated with being connected 24/7 is a daily challenge. It presents unique tests for self-confidence and these pressures are predicted to increase.

The explosion of social media has wrought other unwanted changes; namely ease of access to pornography, spawning actions such as building an on-line score. A young person living out their lives online, attached to their phone 24/7, can feel pressured to send and receive inappropriate video imagery. Spreading fake photos on social media increases the horrendous negative effects on the confidence of an unsuspecting victim once it comes to light.

Cyber-safety experts report that the majority of child exploitation material online is self-generated, with children as young as eight voluntarily posting photos of their private body parts online and proudly showing the pictures at school. In the past, eight-year-olds may have been playing outside, practicing a sport, wrestling their siblings or helping their parents with chores. It's vital to support children in acquiring the confidence to report inappropriate online activity and engage in healthy non-screen actions.

Prior to our technology era, bullying or harassment was limited to personal contact. Once school was over for the day, the victimised person could leave it behind and go home. Nowadays, technology and social media's emphasis on appearance is associated with cyber-bullying. Being connected 24/7 there is no reprieve for the victim. Online cyber-bullying and suicide taunts in extreme cases have been associated with vulnerable children taking their own lives.

Some things haven't changed! Children are still desperate to be older than their chronological years. Young ones are frantic to reach double figures, then it's on to the tweens and early teens.

Competition sports still exist. Children and youth of all ages play team sports at school and on weekends. Playing sport develops confidence emanating from a sense of achievement, belonging and security.

The uniformity of team clothing and the physical effort to participate at a competitive level continues. Consequently, team members, relaxed about clothing, focus on their activity. They may have a crazy socks day or other variation for a fun alternative but dressing in a uniform, they don't have to think about what to wear.

Modern generations

Whereas previous generations spent a couple of decades in the education system, worked in a career, then prepared for retirement, cyber intelligence is the new normal. Together with a probable extended lifespan, the rise of technology impacts development at every stage, from pre-birth analytics to daily life, through each generation. It's entrenched into modern life from birth, right through to almost every action.

Youth don't hold the fear that besets older adults. You may have lost confidence after being censored following posts or comments you made on the internet, thus find you are no longer able to communicate openly on social media . If young people are censored, being so tech-savvy, they soon find a way around it.

Tech entrepreneurs worry that freedom of speech is gradually being eroded and have tried to buy and/or create systems to maintain it. Youth continue as before, none the wiser. They accept as normal the new models of biological engineering, including all developments in medicines, food and materials. They may even try to speed up the ageing process, while at the other end of the spectrum, as an older adult, you do everything to try and slow it down.

Technology alleviates some challenges. People living outside cities can work from home because they can be immediately connected with events and people throughout the nation and across the world. Technological changes to the nature of work, family, culture and values also add stress, not the least of which is due to an expectation that you are constantly available.

Sharing Data

Searching your ancestry and cultural background by submitting your biological data you will have given away the DNA material. As well as providing you with data about your ancestry, the DNA material is used for research, including developing cancer drugs by scientists aiming to understand our functioning, interactions and the regulation of specific genes.

Even blood taken for analysis and replaced with saliva is now a proven option for genomic DNA analysis as the majority of DNA in saliva, coming from your white blood cells, requires no specialised collection and can be frozen and stored.

You may feel thrilled to be a part of something positive in science that could benefit mankind and to find out more about your family history, but the downside is that these collections are not always innocent. A hostile government can use DNA to identify relatives of those citizens who are perceived to step out of line against them, or in developing weapons.

A noted scientist, when being interviewed on radio, explained what's happening with DNA in the world today. In the interview, he also outlined some of the strategic risks of AI, although our children's generation is growing up knowing nothing other than this era of surveillance and espionage. He reminded the audience that technology monitors our every move and DNA is being used as control by countries seeking to track relatives.

By using DNA to trace relatives, a malevolent government can exert control by threatening them, even if the dissenter has left the country. In a democracy, this may seem harmless to you, but we have people in our midst who have settled here to recover their confidence after life under a despotic government. To recuperate, they need a sense that their life here is secure. They acknowledge that there's a risk to a dissident protester upon escaping their country of origin and that data is used to uncover and threaten their relatives back home.

In his interview, the scientist mentioned prenatal tests. They're undertaken by women in Europe, but the results are shipped back to the tester in another country. He highlighted concern that another country had access to the women's DNA. The flow of information is one-way because China absorbs but doesn't ship its data to Europe or the US.

To feel confident that your data is protected, he said we need to de-couple our country from potential risk through the World Wide Web (www). He suggested we need to become independent, monitor technology and be aware of the factors impacting us.

We know social media is not always benign. This knowledge is important for you but more so for the well-being of future generations, especially as there's an increased risk of depression and suicide among children and youth when technology and access to social media are used in excess.

Public opinion, driven by loud, angry minorities whose outrage can be monetised, has stifled discussions in many realms. Social media, from schools to university campuses, driven by X (formerly Twitter), YouTube and Facebook is used to stifle free speech. Governments place bans on big tech companies over 'misinformation'. The inability to openly communicate is potentially destructive to confidence and well-being.

Being aware of the many facets of data sharing is important. Parents and adult caregivers are increasingly aware of the social media company's money-making strategies, including feeding ideas to vulnerable children and youth. But the propaganda through social media and around products and processes is so convincing that adults are vulnerable too.

As a parent or grandparent, you'll be aware of children's and some adults' addiction to iPhones. You'll probably have noticed the meek, compliant, docile children and youth who turned into angry, difficult and even uncontrollable individuals when a parent tries to remove it from them.

Children as young as 10 follow fads on social media, from advertised skin care products to the clothing worn by their idols. They use social media platforms such as TikTok to research images and brands. Constant use of a smartphone to access social media can be a gateway for, and ultimate precursor to, mental health woes.

Like drug and gaming companies, businesses know that profits are made by enticing users to become habitual users of their products. They can bypass parental control because of online connectivity. Children and teens who lack confidence in themselves are especially vulnerable.

Mental health issues and self-harm among our youth have reached such a crisis that governments and health officials are stepping in, declaring the need to restrict and regulate social media use among young people. Confident parents don't want to hand over responsibility for their children to bureaucrats and government officials so they're taking matters into their own hands. This group of parents has likened social media to other at-risk and addictive behaviours and they have launched support groups. They support those who want to delay providing their children access to social media and smartphones.

If you are concerned about bullying, social withdrawal, secretive actions and addiction to devices some suggestions include:

- No phones in the bedroom
- No mobile devices at mealtimes, before school or when doing homework
- Modelling appropriate phone and technology usage by parents
- Robust discussion between children and parents regarding online safety

- Balancing screen time with quality time together without digital distractions

Even top-level athletes aren't immune to online bullying and mental health trauma. For the Paris Olympic Games in 2024, nearly 200 specialist mental health personnel were assigned to help athletes deal with online assaults.

An interviewer asking about the athletes' performances and their mental health and well-being expected these high-performance individuals would be immune to negative commentary and filled with confidence because they'd reached the pinnacle of elite competition in their chosen sport. However, their discussion made the interviewer aware that for the victimised athlete, it's not a simple matter of turning off their social media. Like everyone else, they have every right to use media and to celebrate and promote their success across a range of platforms.

For athletes, it's also a monetised interaction because they depend on sponsors. Thus, they're obliged to build up their image to attract sponsorship deals, so they can't simply turn off. Social media is the ideal platform for them to engage in self-promotion. Until it's not.

A media presence can easily attract the wrong kind of attention and destroy confidence, especially when it can be done anonymously. Personal and/or threats hurt everyone, including elite athletes. It's easy for them and others in the public eye to lose confidence when being stalked or exposed to inflammatory threats from an internet troll whose goal is to elicit a strong emotional response, either for amusement or for another more nefarious intention.

Parenting in a Cyber-World

Constantly using technology means that children, youth and all who use social media are potential targets for online predators. Parents, recognising the inherent dangers of exposing a developing mind to extreme imagery and the power of advertising, as well as potentially malevolent adults who trawl the internet, are questioning at what age it's appropriate to give children mobile technology.

You may decide to wait until your children are 16 before giving them smartphones, hoping they'll have the maturity to deal with the powerful imagery. Others believe it's the responsibility of the software giants to place tighter restrictions on age and the content they're exposed to, or that the government should be involved.

Keeping the lines of communication open between parents, children and teenagers is vital as language and habits change. 'Google' is now a noun, we engage in 'texting', and more recently, 'sexting'. New words arise constantly so parents need each other's support to keep ahead of the game.

The term 'sextortion' has been used to explain exposure to sexualised content and behaviours online. While some parents may be unaware of what their children are consuming online, more are becoming aware of the dangers of grooming by online predators and educating their children about what to do if they're targeted.

Open communication between parents and children is a significant step towards fighting child exploitation. Adults can demonstrate alternatives, such as the goodness and well-being that arise from being connected in face-to-face human interactions.

Tech Giants Limit remember the good times as you look forward to a bright future Their Children's Access

Interestingly, the developers of those same technological systems so popular with our young people, Steve Jobs (co-founder of Apple) and Jonathan Ive (his innovations include the iPod, iMac, MacBook Air, iPhone and iPad) are said to have limited or banned their children from the very tools they created. Others also known worldwide for their technological and engineering developments, Jeff Bezos (founder of Amazon), Bill Gates (co-founder, with Paul Allen, of Microsoft), Mark Zuckerberg (he founded Facebook together with other Harvard University students), Sergey Brin and Larry Page (developers of Google) and Jimmy Wales (co-founder of Wikipedia) all went to Montessori schools, which are anti-tech.

These technology moguls tend to share many of the same qualities, having come from an education system that has an anti-tech philosophy. Many technology workers in Silicon Valley, concerned about mental health and other risks, safeguard their children by sending them to Montessori or similar anti-tech schools where children use pen and paper in classrooms. Technology such as iPhones and computers are banned.

There are rules about no computers at the dinner table and no computers at breakfast. These families and elite schools focus more on building a child's emotional, social and intellectual well-being.

Bill Gates didn't let his children use smartphones until they were 14. Even Taylor

Swift, a darling of modern children and youth, attended a Montessori school for two years. In these circles, there's an understanding that smartphones, social media and other forms of technology can damage young minds. Montessori schools, boasting their preparation of children for all of life, consider that their graduates possess the following range of characteristics:

- Confident, self-aware
- Empathetic, compassionate, kind
- Introspective, questioning
- Eager to learn, possess a love of learning
- Accomplished, capable
- Critical thinkers, independent thinkers
- Creative
- Self-motivated, self-disciplined
- Comfortable with themselves
- Comfortable with adults
- Work cohesively with people of all ages and personalities
- Harmonisers, good citizens

Control of Your Social Media

If your confidence has slipped or you're aware of family members who have taken a dive because of the toxicity or addictive influence of social media, it's time to consider deleting it. Young people themselves, with a Confidage approach, are taking back control of their lives. In a reverse trend, instead of being their guide, adults can learn from them.

If social media is destroying your confidence, you can remove yourself like those young people who have removed themselves and self-assuredly taken back control for the next stage of their lives.

To delete social media from your phone, begin by removing yourself from Twitter (X), and other apps, including Snapchat or Instagram. The hardest is Facebook because it has become so commonplace, along with Messenger, as a means of connectivity and communication.

To remove yourself from Facebook, start manually. Go to the activity log and pick an action such as 'likes'. You'll be amazed when the activity log shows every single thing you have ever liked or reacted to during the years you've been using it. Don't worry about the time you've spent over the years scrolling through Facebook and what you once liked.

Next, you can go ahead and delete 'comments'. Finally, delete 'friends'. Then you'll be ready to close your account. The Confidage advocates who do this find they worry less about appearance and no longer have the urge to take selfies. They have detached from worrying about the views of others. Without being fearful about online exploitation or coming across unwanted violent imagery, life is more peaceful. However, others who don't share this approach are not so fortunate and use the consumption of food as their control mechanism, including many celebrities.

The Importance of Safe Touch

Positive energy and a more helpful style of thinking arise from something as basic as touch. Comfort and security come from human connectivity. The digital world impacts touch because relationships with a plastic screen are not the same. Being stroked or hugged is important to building your confidence, particularly when it comes from someone who cares about you.

Your brain responds to healthy hugs, releasing the feel-good hormones oxytocin, dopamine and serotonin. Without adequate healthy touch, you experience detrimental effects on your health, whereas with hugs, stress is reduced. Studies have shown that babies thrive when held but fail to develop physically and psychologically without touch.

If you observe confident children, you'll note that they engage in physical touching through tussling with siblings and friends, romping around patting animals or enjoying a bedtime cuddle from mum or dad. Engaging with a screen blocks out human connectivity.

There's power in healthy touching. Adults need to nurture and connect deeply with their children. Our fear-based world sees a withdrawal of touch, negating one of the easiest ways to offer love and reassurance. Safe touching is reduced nowadays because of fear of predatory actions, especially those targeting young people.

Healthy intimate relationships need respectful communication, but a byproduct of the devastating stories of violation of children, especially by authority figures, is that the very guidelines designed to protect them have created fear about touch. Abused, they turn to their screens, but those interactions aren't necessarily healthy.

Children need to be educated about safe touching. Most of the people who sexually molest children are known to them, not strangers, so in this highly sexualised world, children need the tools to understand safe touching. As an adult, you can demonstrate sensitivity and respect for children's rights to reject touch if they feel uncomfortable.

Many teenagers, embroiled in their cyber-world, experience a dearth of touch. Excessive consumption of technology, children left unsupervised by busy adults, and living indoors more than being in nature all lead to the loss of awareness of our senses.

Working with adolescents as a school psychologist, my observations and knowledge of school families led me to conclude that aggression and inappropriate behaviour at school, especially among younger adolescent boys, were associated with touch deprivation.

I was always mindful of the need to maintain a safe physical distance from the teenagers in my consulting room due to professional guidelines. Knowing the importance of touch to a child who is crying, I was sorry that the rules and regulations constraining our interactions meant I could not reach out to physically comfort an upset, tearful young person.

To overcome the need for a hug in these situations, I invited one or more of (usually a girl) her chosen friends into our sessions. Their comforting touch soothed their friend. They found relief through touch, by hugging each other, while I remained at a distance.

Each child and adolescent will have a certain preference around safe touch. The fact that humans are not meant to be alone, separate from others, illustrates the link between the absence of loving care in early life and distress among adults.

Adults, like children and teenagers, seek intimacy and a close sense of belonging in order to feel valued. Feeling sensorily deprived through being constantly online and/or limited to conversations via a screen, you may opt for a massage or appointment with a hairdresser – treatments based on safe touch.

In communities that live with high touch, everyone thrives. There are few of the mental health concerns that plague our children, youth and the elderly in those places.

We all feel safe and secure knowing that there's someone who will provide gentle touch when we need to be comforted. Therefore, we must consider how to build more safe touch within our homes.

Maybe your young children find their way into your bed in the middle of the night because they're frightened. This is your cue to soothe them. If their squirming and wriggling interrupts your sleep, once they're settled, go to their bed. Gentle touch builds comfort and confidence as long as the adult exerts no pressure and awaits tacit approval from the young person before touching them. Aware adults positively help children develop inner strength, resilience and confidence.

Cyber-Developments

We are yet to determine the role of AI as we move forward in the realm of connectivity and associated technological augmentations. Given that robotics is developing at an accelerated rate, we don't know yet what this will mean for confidence.

For example, gaming, another technological change industry, has been added to the career structure of course offerings at university. But in other countries, gaming isn't restricted to a university degree. In Denmark, it's already studied in schools and they have developed a strong culture of competitive gaming, supporting players from an early age. Their ESports are celebrated, motivating players with confidence to achieve success in a new frontier, so watch this space.

Technology involves so many developments it's hard to predict the next trend. One recent idea – to insert chips into your body, hands, even your brain – can seem very scary. Knowing too much information too quickly can be negative and the pitch begins in incremental steps, such as facial recognition. It's already been very convincing. Are you one of the many people who have embraced every new development on your smartphone due to convenience?

The downside is that those who are spending billions trying to manipulate you are also exposing you to unthinkingly accepting AI and a digital future. You may agree to accept changes so you get better photos without worrying if your camera is tracking your eye movements and watching all the people near you. You may not be concerned that your computer captures all your keystrokes and records the patterns of your life.

If it does impact your confidence, you can choose to exert your personal power. But it takes great courage to turn your back on digital control when it's so convenient. Knowing that biometric control can't happen if you maintain real connections with real people, you can choose whether or not you want to live in the real world or a digital world for the sake of convenience.

Cyber-developments are so rapid that the interwoven realities between cyber-life and real-life are being jumbled. We live in an era where we all use computers often, for work or daily communication, so we're constantly seeing ourselves on a screen. We interact with recipients by speaking to each other's images. Seeing ourselves on screen continuously makes us hyper-critical. Our face and body are objectified and we judge how others see us. Technology gives rise to facial recognition so there is a constant emphasis on seeing our face. It makes it easier for some everyday actions, and sharing data is useful but only if it enhances, not detracts, from your confidence.

Assertiveness

Vulnerability leaves you open to manipulation. One way to avoid being a target for psychological operators, propaganda and malevolent cyber-hackers is to be vigilant and more assertive. Behaving assertively isn't the same as being aggressive. Maybe you reached your current age without knowing the differences between aggression and assertive actions.

When you're dealing with the inevitable challenges of technology, you need to stand up for yourself. Have you unknowingly adopted aggression or assertiveness, frustration or patience with the many technologies you are required to use on a daily basis? Note how you behave around these inanimate objects. If you're sometimes frustrated, you are not alone. Even the most tech-savvy have their moments.

The freedom to express your feelings doesn't necessarily mean you get your own way. It does mean *not* holding onto negative or aggressive feelings. If you bury your feelings because you're frightened to express yourself, the feelings turn inward and can turn toxic and/or fill you with anxiety and fear.

Assertiveness means you can say what's on your mind without taking responsibility for how other people respond. You don't have to be a doormat and do everything someone else says to do because you worry about conflict. Whatever your age and stage of life, it's time to ditch self-limiting beliefs and have honest, assertive conversations.

You're not responsible for the way others think or what they say about you or anyone else. You're only responsible for the way you behave and how you treat others. If you have lived life being hostile or aggressive, it can be easy to self-sabotage when you're feeling inadequate around technology. Practice being assertive when you need help.

Businesses listened. The older generation and people with disabilities were feeling frustrated and angry that technology wasn't suited to them so manufacturers responded.

They devised a solution aimed at the target group. Instead of the first mobile phones with their tiny buttons and touch screen display, manufacturers created larger screens, enabling everyone to be connected and to manage social and other media minus the frustration; a win-win all around.

Being more aware of what you want and need to make your life easier is made more difficult if you haven't been an assertive person but there's no better time to learn new ways. If you let go of unnecessary baggage, technological or otherwise, you can spend more time on self-nurturing activities and stand up politely for what you want and need.

Others who know you may at first be surprised, even shocked, by the newly assertive you. They may take time to adjust to your self-confidence as you say what you think and act accordingly. If they respond strangely, don't worry. Remember how negative, self-limiting beliefs made you feel? Like everything, it takes practice. Notice the improvement in your mood when you're being more assertive.

Technology and social media have many positive uses. World events, sport, politics and human-interest stories are easily spread through access to the internet. But the government's attempts to impose sanctions on social media through a Disinformation Bill can challenge your freedom and leave you feeling helpless, as happened to Gary.

Gary's Discomfort About Future Technology

Gary, a mature man in his late 60s, was worried by discussions about a fourth industrial revolution and the possibility of being implanted with a silicon chip to induce a form of humanism never before seen.

A member of the Baby Boomer generation, he had a grasp of historical developments but the recent information he'd gained from social media left him feeling uncomfortable and uncertain about the future. As a new grandfather, he told me he was horrified when he saw members at the World Economic Forum (WEF) outline an intention to transform our very humanity.

Expecting the freedom to choose new activities in retirement and the time to do the things he'd put off in the past due to competing demands, when the government required us to stay at home following their announcement of a worldwide pandemic in 2020, Gary used his time to view content on social media.

The WEF reports dinted his confidence. He feared a chip being implanted in his wrist, which would link all aspects of his identity. He described images of 'google' glass that turned our eyeballs into a computer, and discussed a future where we'd walk around with virtual reality headsets, living in an alternative reality. Gary's fears about the future were not for himself. His main concern was the world to be inhabited by his grandchild and any future grandchildren. He was worried that, in a life already dominated by screens and devices, information about their every move could be extracted by an external force with malicious intentions.

His thoughts took him to some dark places but I assured him he wasn't the only grandparent to experience these concerns. He acknowledged that the younger generation is tech-dependent, thus his children and grandchildren absorbed each new development merely as a natural progression along a continuum.

Gary's fear and psychological distress impacted his inner confidence. As a Baby Boomer, he felt his life wouldn't last long enough to feel the impact of the WEF agenda but he was concerned for his family's future. To cope with his fears, he'd become very involved in research, using the internet to uncover various sources and data. This enabled him to be more confident about the technology but, in trying to pass on his findings to family members, he created a wedge between them.

In order to restore his family relationships, we decided he needed to set some boundaries around how much time he spent on multiple social media sites. He also considered with whom he could discuss his revelations, agreeing to avoid conversations about global issues and politics with his family. He extended this ban to incorporate some friends. He'd felt hurt that they'd laughingly labelled him an unhinged conspiracy theorist because, in his work as a scientist-practitioner, he'd been well-regarded for the quality of his research and known for the evidence he produced.

On becoming more confident, he decided to join groups of like-minded people through social media. Once he restricted the sharing of his ideas and findings to similar like-minded group members, he was able to visit his grandchildren and interspersed his time with family and friends conversing about other matters.

Your confidence can be tied to the actions of others, but as Gary learnt, it's essential to maintain important relationships and carefully select with whom to discuss controversial matters. Spending more time with his grandchild and helping the parents, he found that it was being with close family and friends that provided his greatest joy and fulfilment.

Helping out parents by looking after the grandchildren has a two-fold purpose. In Gary's case, it gave him meaning and purpose. He enjoyed being included in their world. When his grandchildren asked questions and showed an interest in his life, he felt imbued with purpose, thus his confidence was renewed.

Chapter Five

Whatever your experiences, age or life stage, your life stories contain a personal philosophical richness, allowing you to contribute confidently to your own life and that of others you know. The hurry to reach adulthood keeps us ever busier as we move through the life stages until we find ourselves at an age when we want the birthdays to stop.

We were all young once, with elastic skin, not wrinkles, and minus the effects of gravity pulling everything lower. Consciously confident, when you're happy in your skin, you value the beauty within all of us. Maturity brings more understanding of each life stage.

It's rewarding to reflect on and celebrate your life. It takes effort to create, deal with and/or manage life confidently. When you acknowledge your feelings, you can deal with them. Confidence helps.

Fear Saps Your Energy

We are all subject to fear at times. It's an important aspect of the fight or flight instinct and necessary for survival. But fear driven by war, governments, the media and individual personality factors can be limiting. There's been no requirement to join the military and defend our country for several generations, but you may be judgmental about those who focus on their individual needs and wants rather than the good of the country.

Maybe you or your parents were among the common radical leftist students whose fears saw you at rallies against the war in Vietnam and embracing the peace movements of the 1960s. The themes from previous generations may have changed but youth rebellion remains one of the normal passages to a mature life. Fear and boredom still drive social movements.

Today's university students are prey to helicopter parenting and hyper-safety alarmism driven by fear. COVID-19 and the ongoing focus on potential illnesses, together with worldwide conflicts, such as those between Russia/Ukraine and Israel/Palestine exacerbate fear. Young people today are often terrified about their economic future or captive to climate alarmism. Thinking that they will catch some awful disease, that homeownership and the lifestyle of their parents and grandparents is unattainable, that their home will sink under the weight of floods or burn down in a bushfire, it's easier to focus on what they can do to change what they look like. That's perhaps the only thing they feel they can control.

Without health or someone to care for you, everyone is vulnerable to distress. When you take your health for granted and it's taken from you, your security is thrown. Even figures as well-known as the King of England and Catherine, the Princess of Wales are not immune to poor health. When she unexpectedly developed cancer, Catherine disappeared from public view as her treatment forced her to withdraw from public life for a considerable period of time. She said it presented her family with an unanticipated health scare and it prompted her to reassess her priorities.

If you suffer ill health or a relationship breakdown during your early forties, a time when you hold responsible roles while trying to secure your financial future, it can be devastating. Feeling your options diminishing, you may feel forced into new behaviours that deplete your energy.

Insecurity can result, driving you further into the cosmetics and fitness industry. Some women and men, after failed relationships and/or failed marriages, become even more intent on making physical changes to their appearance in the belief that it's necessary to compete with other younger women or fitter, more 'ripped' muscular Adonis-like males.

You may have left a relationship because a partner wore you out with his/her constant demands for excessive admiration, but now you're fearful that your options are diminishing.

Has your fear to look eternally youthful been so overwhelming that you've forgotten your chronological age and how to relax? Maybe fear resulted in you accompanying your child to a nightclub, with patrons mistakenly thinking you are her/his partner but when you've been invited to take various substances by the much younger attendees, all you've wanted to do is go home, make a cup of tea and go to bed. Fear is such a strong emotion that it may govern your belief that relationships will be successful if only you change.

Maybe you're a woman who has been so badly traumatised in a former relationship(s) that you no longer trust men. Nor do you trust other women. If they represent rivals or see you as one, is the only person you feel comfortable with a much older man? Do you feel safe with him because he represents a father figure and you feel comforted with the hope that he will rescue you? If you don't think you're worthy of affection from someone your own age, do you try even more desperately to hide behind false bravado with people in the workplace and end up moving from job to job? Feeling left out socially, do you adopt a fighting stance with the world around you before it can hurt you?

Can you relate to the near-perfect face of the woman who awakens on a particular birthday feeling no longer beautiful but instead worried she is fat, ugly or unwanted? Are you this woman, the one who envies her husband as he continues his morning routine untroubled by his physical body while you're trapped by fear?

Are you focused on things you think have bypassed you now that your body directs your thinking to blemishes and physical frailties? Are you terrified that you're not equipped to accept losing your image of perfection and worried about being ill-prepared for changes to your body in physical strength and capacity?

Fear and reality cause you to reassess your security, lifestyle and the future. Each stage of life brings challenges – some good and others you wish you never had to experience. However, if you've wasted time by always comparing yourself with others while busily working and raising a family you'll be on a never-ending merry-go-round. Fearing physical challenges or distressed due to loneliness or isolation, you may lose sight of your business or life direction.

Have you been operating, subconsciously or otherwise, out of fear and doubt, not fully trusting yourself and allowing others to influence or make your decisions? Maybe you've been influenced by too many external forces without realising it. There's always time to begin making changes, large or small, and to stand on your own two feet.

If this means taking a new life direction don't be disheartened by the responses you get from others. It can be daunting to face erstwhile colleagues, friends and family and explain your new ideas and ideals. It's unnerving initially for anyone when undertaking new habits and it takes time to develop a non-fearful trajectory.

Look for new sources of energy. Build on your existing and new resources. Having chosen to move in a new direction, you may need to simplify aspects of your old life. This doesn't mean letting go of everything and everyone important to you. Retain your core values and beliefs but let go of fearful thinking, including worry about being hurt.

Thoughts Count

Permit yourself a moment to listen to your thoughts. Did you think that with willpower and money, you would overcome any obstacle and now you beat yourself up with guilty thoughts that you have somehow failed because you haven't reached particularly lofty heights? If so, you need to change or replace this automatic negative self-talk or worry-thinking. Guilt is the preserve of those who commit atrocious acts and deliberately seek to harm another. That doesn't apply to you. These are just thoughts and no one knows what you're thinking unless you tell them.

Changing your thoughts and becoming more confident can occur at any age. The main thing is not to think you're guilty if you don't comply with perceived expectations from other sources.

You can relax once you give up the struggle of thinking you must look younger to prove your competence and worth. You don't have to please anyone else or succumb to fear. When not consumed by thoughts that you must meet someone else's expectations you are freer to enjoy your own company, say what you like, eat what you like (within reason), do everything or do nothing.

If you're at the stage of life when you have no more responsibilities for children, you may be worrying about being lonely once they move out. Instead of worry-thinking, imagine happy thoughts, such as joy that they're getting on with their lives as part of the natural order.

Once you're no longer spending time trying to prove yourself competent to a boss or on efforts you make to attract a potential partner, you're free to think about other matters. Nearing retirement or reaching your late 60s or 70s, you may think your memory is changing. What if, instead of worrying about it, you thought 'My forgetfulness is natural because my mind is currently on overload'?

If you've moved and find yourself in an unfamiliar environment, think about what you can do to manage your new environment. If you've lost a partner, whilst it can be tragic, don't stay mired in negative thoughts for too long. Without your partner with whom to go rock climbing, ride a surfboard or climb metaphorical and real mountains, your thoughts can immobilise you.

If you are alone, you may feel doomed to a life of loneliness. Spending too much time being introspective predisposes you to negative thoughts about your health. It's worse if you've been living with an unspoken promise to yourself – namely, thinking that if you do the right thing with your body and health you will have everlasting love with a significant partner for life.

Maybe you're feeling fragile because now you're alone, you're more aware of ageing. Or perhaps you've partnered with someone narcissistic, arrogant or self-centred and you're blaming yourself, thinking it must be aspects of your personality that attracted the wrong person.

Have you asked a partner or friends to tell you if there's something about you that they don't like, thinking that it may boost your self-confidence? Maybe your self-esteem was fragile and you were expecting positive reinforcement about how special you were to them. However, sometimes jealousy results in gaslighting, with responses couched in such a way that you doubt yourself and your self-assurance is dented.

It doesn't often happen that such a question elicits an uncomfortable response as friends and partners are more likely to be kind to one another, but the consequences for your self-esteem can be horrifying if they're unkind. Even the strongest of us can experience jealousy, but when directed at you by someone you trust, it can be destructive.

Because you were not expecting it, brutal honesty that's unexpectedly cruel can strip your confidence. Be wary of thinking others will do and say what you expect.

On the other hand, if your circumstances change but you're pleased with your life choices and the friendships you've made, you may be filled with confidence and decide to plunge into new challenges. Value yourself. Know inherently that you are a good person, not limited by your thoughts. Choose helpful thoughts and embrace whatever stage of life you inhabit. Look to your 50s, 60s and beyond with pleasure.

It's how you think about yourself that is paramount to how you feel. Maybe, like Mark, you thought you needed to be perfect.

Mark: Sabotaged by Perfectionism

I met Mark in an interview because he wanted to get his life back on track. Mark's story began when he felt the need to move out of a toxic home environment as soon as he finished Year 12. His family's behaviour left him feeling drained so he thought he'd be better alone.

Once on his own with no family support, he was forced to survive at a subsistence level. His income was limited to the casual and part-time work he managed to scrounge. To put a roof over his head, he had to depend on his friends' generosity. He slept on their couches as he didn't have enough salary or savings to pay even for the rental of a single room. He became quite depressed and lost the last shreds of his self-confidence.

This all changed when he met a special girl. They developed a loving, empathic, mutually supportive relationship. She nurtured his dreams about entering university and helped him obtain a student allowance. He successfully gained entry to a course and managed to keep his part-time job as well. When combined, his salary and student allowance enabled him to rent a room from his girlfriend's mother.

Their relationship settled, his accommodation needs sorted, studying an interesting course and making some money from working, Mark enjoyed life again. He and his girlfriend lived and studied together. Both achieved strong academic results. He was proud that he'd turned his life around and felt confident about how he was moving forward.

'Everything was going so well. I was really looking forward to my final year. I knew there would be heaps of assignments, but I had things well organised and couldn't wait to complete my studies and move into a worthwhile career. But then it all fell apart. My girlfriend and I broke up and now I can't seem to get on top of anything. Of course I had to move out. I've had to work more shifts in my casual job to keep up with the rent of a room at a new place and I'm falling way behind with assignments. I can't see how I can do anything other than drop out, but that thought fills me with dread as I know that will make me even more of a disappointment to my father,' he bemoaned.

Despite being so near his goal, due to his changed circumstances, Mark's self-doubt returned with a thud and his confidence plummeted. Whereas he'd been excitedly looking toward the future, his failed relationship impacted his whole mood and well-being. He ruminated about not being good enough, blaming himself for ever being taken in by thinking he could make it in his chosen career or that he could create a life better than he'd experienced as a child.

Finally tired from talking, Mark sat back to listen. We outlined some activities to help him recognise and manage his idealised image and the pros and cons of setting exceedingly high standards, his attempts to be 'perfect' and its effect on his confidence.

He acknowledged that he'd been driving himself so hard to deal with disappointment and realised he was repeating the patterns of his father. He described a self-critical man who judged others on their performance and yet who procrastinated to the extent that he rarely completed tasks. Like his father, Mark had been excessively concerned with how others saw him and he was exhausted by trying to live up to his perception of his father's expectations.

Having become more aware of how his perfectionism was fueled by habitual negative thoughts, I introduced a mindfulness practice. We located a web-based resource and agreed that it was an important strategy but required practice if he was to make use of it when dealing with his personal stress. By the time we'd finished, Mark had a clear sense of purpose and realistic strategies. He agreed to practice and suggested we should follow up for the next couple of weeks.

When he returned for our fourth meeting, Mark's gait on entering the room had changed. He walked erectly, with head held high and shoulders back, giving him an air of confidence. I commented on his demeanor and he reported that he'd made positive progress. His mindfulness practice was working and because he was more relaxed, he'd become more interested in study again. He'd renewed his goals and had a purpose.

Through talking to me for several weeks, doing online research about letting go of perfectionism and being more involved with mindfulness practices, Mark salvaged his motivation and confidence. In time, he presented as a confident young man. He'd developed less self-punitive thinking and behaviour. Rather than drop out as he had initially proposed, upon knowing how his old habit of perfectionism made him vulnerable, he committed to continue mindfulness and redeemed his career focus.

Mark came to see me three years later to share his success. He was proud to report that he was in a great career and maintained his conscious decision not to let perfectionism drive him to the point of exhaustion. He had a relaxed, enjoyable social life with few demands but there was a girl in whom he had a special interest.

Identifying why he'd developed a perfectionist habit and how it impeded his well-being and by making different choices, Mark's story ended positively. There are many more for whom the challenges of living with a punitive, toxic or hostile family of origin have a different outcome.

Troubled Youth

Feeling insecure, unloved and unsafe, many young people seek out gang membership. They think it will provide safety, enhance their status among friends and reward them with a sense of belonging.

The environments of youth who become affiliated with gangs are usually the more extreme. Temporary excitement from making money by selling drugs and other illegal activities may imbue a sense of camaraderie and boldness, but it doesn't necessarily translate into self-confidence.

Youth crime waves are gripping many cities. Our governments are increasingly focussed on crimes committed by young people in Australia. It's difficult for authorities to prioritise which intervention and prevention programs most suit at-risk children. It's recognised that they need strategies to build healthier self-esteem if they are to withstand the pressures and make more helpful choices. Many entrepreneurial people are devising programs that have the support of governments as they try to stem the recidivism rate.

We each develop positive self-regard or self-confidence in different ways due to differing experiences, expectations, environments and habits, including perfectionism. We can attribute or blame our emotional personality and other inherited characteristics on our family of origin, society, the community or the culture into which we are born. A young person's brain is not developed enough to assess information or understand threats and risks in the same way as adults.

Growing up with low self-esteem in an environment devoid of positive role models and support, gang membership may seem an alluring choice. Although adolescents and even younger children who lack confidence and feel marginalised have been recruited into gangs, very few are born into them.

Widely divergent risk factors impact on building confidence, including low educational aspiration, commitment and attainment, together with high levels of anti-social behaviour, family instability, violence, drugs and mental health issues. Maturity enables us to recognise actions and choices, both conscious and unconscious, and how they fit our values.

Despite our circumstances, financial realities and deprivations, with care from significant others, we can be confident about our place in the world. Children who grow up in a loving home are more likely to spend a carefree childhood and become confident adults.

Those lucky enough to grow up in a rural environment prior to the internet and the technology boom instinctively developed an understanding of important matters of life and death by observing the natural world. Children watching their fathers and mothers tend to all their animals, managing through droughts, floods and the other day-to-day experiences for people on the land and their families, learn about nature and overcoming adversity with support and hard work. Living through difficulties, they learn that actions have consequences, so resilience is born.

Traditionally, coming-of-age in Australia often incorporated a stint in the bush as a jackeroo or jillaroo. Stations and properties offered school leavers farm experiences. This pipeline of young people led some to a successful career in agriculture. Today's youth are more inclined to got to Schoolies celebrations in Surfer's Paradise or similar after completing their schooling.

Given the youth crime issues, one strategy to help troubled city youth develop positive alternative behaviours has been to take them back to basics on the land. Working with animals and experiencing the soft and harsh conditions in nature empowers confidence. Animals don't care what you look like or what you wear. They respond to kindness and are non-judgmental.

Born in Darwin and raised in Alice Springs to a Warlpiri mother and Anglo-Celtic father, Senator Jacinta Nampijinpa Price provided a positive example of the effect of nature and nurture. Her main concern as a child whenever tragedy struck was her parents' well-being. This was the result of having lost a brother to leukemia when she was three.

Resilient in the face of loss and the difficulties of life in the Northern Territory, Senator Price is a positive role model. She's raised four sons of Mauritian, Warlpiri, Malay Indian, Chinese, Scots, Irish, Welsh, Scandinavian, African and German heritage, and her main source of pride is, as she says 'above all they are modern Australia'.[8]

Uncovering the personal stories of others, you'll find all of us are challenged to some degree by a constantly changing world and stressors particular to contemporary Australians regardless of where you live or how old you are. Whatever your age, life journey or events along the way, things are not nearly as daunting if you share them.

Increasingly complicated work demands and the pace of life have become more stressful for everybody. No one is immune. From the doctors and psychologists who help people manage their health and confidence to the

CEO or the janitor, the rapid pace of life and its accompanying complications contribute to distress and can attack self-confidence.

Expectations – your own or those thrust on you – may further augment distress and impact your confidence and well-being. If you're stressed, anxious and/or depressed and feel your confidence seeping away, you're not alone! In fact, history reveals that you are in the company of many famous people worldwide, past and present, who have lived with psychological distress conditions prevalent among the general adult population.

You might be surprised at how many – from ordinary people to famous icons – worry and feel insecure about their looks, their relationships and not being good enough. If you're to overcome these insecurities, it's important to recognise and manage negative thinking, and that imperfections are accepted and low self-esteem is conquered.

Some famous role models who had to overcome insecurities include Naomi Campbell, who, growing up, worried about her skin until she acknowledged the importance of accepting her body at any age. Kim Kardashian was depressed about her curves until her father helped her change her thinking and love her body.

Jennifer Lopez, insecure about her voice, worried that other singers would judge her, while Joan Rivers' daughter revealed her mother's insecurities based on looks, age and being overlooked by others until, fearless on stage, she overcame her insecurity.[9]

Globalisation increasingly connects generations of people across the planet. It enables the sharing of ideas from people in the entertainment industry to professional practice and within social and government circles as well as among people of different cultures and societies. The world you inhabit is now considered a global village.

As you leave the child-rearing years behind and progress through the mid-years to retirement, views on life and opportunities are similar among adults in the Western world. So are the challenges. There's no dearth of research about children, adolescents, young people and the elderly but there's little research on the mid-stages except for data regarding gender and career. It's easier to study those in child care centres, schools, universities or aged-care facilities than among the wider community of mid-life individuals.

Many factors, including whether or not you reach maturity feeling confident, impact your arrival at the midpoint of life. If you're plagued by anxious thoughts, you may ascribe blame to your family of origin, the workplace environment, peers, relationships the system or your age. However, anxiety has no age limits as Sasha explains.

Sasha's Anxiety

For the 15 years Sasha was married, she never attended her husband's business functions. She thought they had an unwritten rule that he keep his work separate from their family life. When he unexpectedly invited her to go to a dinner with him following a major work promotion, at first she refused. However, he was insistent. Unable to come up with a reasonable excuse, although terrified, she finally agreed.

As the days passed, plagued with insecurity about having a less-than-perfect figure compared to the wives she expected to meet, she focussed on how many extra gym sessions she would need to fit in before the event if she was to look presentable according to her impossibly high standards. Once she'd programmed additional sessions, she then berated herself about having nothing to wear that fitted her or to match the occasion.

She worried that she wouldn't have enough time to go to the hairdresser on the day and was anxious about the length of time needed to fashion her hair into an appropriate style. These continuous fears about her overall appearance paralysed her and once her husband left for work, Sasha froze into inactivity for the day. She sat with a cup of coffee, deliberating what to do. Overwhelmed by indecision, she did nothing for hours on end.

As the date drew closer, she spent her evenings reading up on fashion in magazines. Finally, she was motivated enough to book a hairdressing appointment after completing her final round of gym sessions. Despite being physically fit, coiffed and showered, when the evening arrived, clothes strewn all over the bed in her efforts to find the correct dress, Sasha was stricken by a lack of confidence and hesitancy.

Tired of waiting, her husband came upstairs to see what was taking so long. Due to her anxiety, she feigned a headache, telling him she couldn't come after all because she was unwell and had nothing to wear. Seeing the disarray and knowing her as he did, he recognised her fears. He persuaded her to drink some water then gently managed to select a dress and help her get ready.

Sasha attended the function but insisted it could never happen again. She finally broke down in front of her husband. Knowing that her anxiety had reached a new low, he offered encouragement and support as she accepted his suggestion that she undergo some therapy. Once she'd confided in him, Sasha was so relieved, and her path to well-being began.

He went with her for the first few sessions and after a series of sessions alone, Sasha successfully addressed her fears about ageing and appearance. At a deeper level, she came to understand the underlying issues from her childhood that had impacted on her confidence and how it translated into irrational behaviours aimed at helping her reach and maintain an impossible ideal.

Sasha's anxiety and lack of confidence is not confined to one gender. It's as typical among males as it is among women. This is demonstrated in the following snapshot of Tony's experiences.

Tony Manages Anxious Feelings

A 55-year-old man named Tony regularly met with a group of retired and semi-retired executives, all male. In this group setting, he experienced men behaving badly to each other, and especially towards him.

These men had been directors in similar industries to Tony's, although each had worked at different organisations. They'd joined as a group when they recognised each other as the same men who regularly swam and/or walked each morning at the same time on the same beach. They became further acquainted when, after the walk, they met at a beachside café. After their breakfast, most of the group left for work or to catch up with their wives for the day's activities. Except Tony. No longer working, with no wife to go home to, Tony went home alone.

He described feeling lost. He thought he'd enjoy early retirement but realised as he farewelled the men to their places of work and/or wives, he felt as empty as the apartment to which he returned each day.

When one of the men invited Tony to attend a function with another group of men, all of whom held powerful positions in industry at their monthly meetings to discuss investment opportunities, Tony was initially delighted. He felt a renewed sense of purpose.

However, he hadn't realised how far his confidence had sunk since he'd been out of the workforce and in the intervening years since his divorce. Early retirement had left him feeling less important than the others. He questioned what they thought of him.

This level of worry spread to his other social situations. He began to second-guess what friends and family thought of him. Caught in a cycle of helplessness, this formerly successful executive overdid gym sessions, thinking it would add to his appeal but it only resulted in him sustaining an injury.

Previously, he'd covered up his lack of confidence by keeping extraordinarily busy with work and he'd told himself he didn't need a woman in his life since he'd left the marriage years before. In retirement, any relationships within the new group environment soured as he spiralled into depressive thinking. He was caught up in a vicious circle because the less he contributed, the more he was excluded and his confidence plummeted.

It took many sessions of self-reflection for him to understand that his desire to be perfect had provided an extremely successful business model and a good payout from his company but left him feeling unwanted.

Therapy helped him to change his thinking and adapt with practice to more helpful behaviours. As he began to enjoy the meetings, he found the unexpected pay-off was an improved social life.

From there, he developed a special relationship with a family friend. This mature woman had been recently widowed, but because he'd known her a long time, he didn't see it as dating. He wanted to help her to deal with the loss of her husband who'd also been his friend. He felt comfortable and because it was a long-term family friendship, he found it easy to be authentic. He didn't have to try to present a perfect image or to embellish his past. The more relaxed he was, the stronger the relationship and this applied to the group of men with whom he swam and breakfasted as well.

It took time and practice, but once Tony let go of unrealistic expectations, he enjoyed renewed confidence with everyone. He had a renewed sense of purpose and approached his future positively.

Are you caught up in the cycle of obsessing about what has happened in the past? Are you incessantly predicting what might happen in the future? Like Sasha and Tony, understanding the impact of your anxious thoughts about things that have already happened will not change the past. Nor will worrying about the future because it's not here yet and worrying about it will impact your body.

As Sasha and Tony found, feelings can be scary and difficult. But in reading their stories, you'll note it's possible to be more open and relaxed when released from worry about keeping up appearances.

To keep pace as you develop greater confidence, it's been suggested that you keep a journal to serve as a record of your developing knowledge and changes as you progress through this book. Re-reading your journal entries provides insights into your evolving thoughts, feelings and behaviours and any stress management strategies that have been especially helpful in maintaining your confidence as you age.

Try recording your responses to the following activity:

- Confident or anxious: who am I? how do I see myself – e.g. responsible or helpless?
- Childhood memories: what do I remember others saying about me? S(h)e's trouble/brilliant/just like me/like your family?
- What were your early learning, modelling and experiences and how have they impacted on the way you dress, walk/talk and/or your behaviour choices?
- As a teenager – a time when bodies change – we become focussed on gaining peer acceptance. In adolescence, we're in more contact with peers and our interactions with family members declines as we seek peers for self-validation as well as companionship. Desperate for acceptance, we know

of youth who have joined gangs and engaged in inappropriate and/or illegal behaviours. What was it like for you?

- List all the current challenges you think exist that may have impacted on the development of self-confidence among people you know from friends, family and colleagues to acquaintances. Look through the list and identify the common factors and those that you believe are specific to you.

- Has your lack of confidence been exacerbated by loneliness?

- Think about the media and the images you hold and whether or not this has impacted on your confidence and self-esteem.

- In what way do you consider that the pace of life contributes to distress and lack of confidence?

- Check if your self-talk about your place in the world, and your childhood memories of what others said about you in your family of origin (e.g. s(h)e's trouble/brilliant, just like me/like your family) are helpful and if not, what happens if you let go?

- If you can identify genetic links from the family between your confidence and anxiety, and/or experiences impacting negatively on your dress, walk, talk or behaviour choices, select the bits you want to keep or work on and what you'll discard.

If you find yourself clenching your fists, jaw or teeth, breathing rapidly or sweating, take some time to sit quietly. When you're are anxious, you unconsciously breathe more rapidly, taking only shallow breaths, so it's important to focus on deepening your breath. You could count to three as you breathe in, hold it for three, then breathe out slowly as you count again. Try it a few times until you feel your body becoming limp and loose.

You can't take back the past, nor can you control a future that has not yet arrived. All you can do is focus on the present and relax your body and mind.

Changed Work and Living Conditions

Times have never been more competitive, socially and in the workforce. This may add to your stress. An industrial revolution followed the agricultural era and now we're faced with rapid technological change and political instability.

Technological Advances

Technological advances and communication infrastructure enable us to do everything faster, including work. AI is increasingly incorporated into more of our everyday tools for living. It changes the way work gets done and is especially challenging for women and those employed in the more routine tasks as these are the sectors most prone to being displaced by technology. However, no profession is immune from AI. Lawyers, doctors, other professionals and businesses are holding conversations about how AI can be incorporated into their daily practice.

You're forced to do commerce, make airline or other bookings online and pay bills using the internet or a smartphone. The changes have been incremental, especially since the pandemic resulted in more people working from home.

The Office

The office was a place where you made friends, working with others you saw on a daily basis provided a ready-made community. Lunching with colleagues enabled people to meet up at the water cooler, and being in the workplace contributed to wellness. Relationships formed among and via office employees.

Today, even if you operate in a hybrid situation, empty offices limit socialising at work as people's hours in the building no longer necessarily coincide. Employees demanding more flexibility with virtual offices have changed the rhythms of life and large companies are getting bigger and bigger, gobbling up everything in their wake. Employees are prizing security and days away from the office over fulfilment from the job. Loyalty to an employer has changed, with Millennials' work ethic tied to climate change, employee satisfaction and entitlements.

Educational Environments

Educational environments, as well as workplaces, have changed since COVID-19. Tertiary students, once enjoying a busy university community, are increasingly 'meeting' online. This changes relationships.

If you're a student, especially of a mature age, you may not feel comfortable sharing experiences with younger educational peers about the demands of academia, writing assignments, sitting tests and meeting deadlines if not meeting face-to-face. You may be even less comfortable about sharing personal details such as what it's like to have a family member or close friend suffering from a mental health condition or your qualms about facing the demands of a new career.

Mental Health

Mental health is associated with social connectivity. Current post-pandemic working conditions and continuous workforce reductions result in decreased socialisation, so when it comes to study, career and/or mental health, you may feel alone. The accelerating pace of life in the 21st century is stressful but some stigma around mental health remains.

Perhaps you won't admit to anxiety or depression in case it has negative career or relationship repercussions or because you don't think others would empathise and understand how you feel. If you're worried for yourself or someone close to you, help is available in the first instance through Lifeline[10] or Beyond Blue[11]. It takes courage to make the first step but without help, the alternative may be serious.

Courage requires confidence. It's okay to ask for help, whether or not you are a young or mature-aged student. Have you experienced the difficulty of going against one's peer group? It's especially awkward when competing with the hormonal and other aspects of puberty and adolescence or the power of government. Maybe you went against the tide as a teenager or more recently you rebelled against the global and Western government's pandemic lock-down, mask-wearing or vaccination narrative?

Threatened by restrictive government practices, confident or desperate individuals have engaged in uprisings to the exclusion of their mental health. For example, in 2014, tens of thousands of courageous activists, including almost all university students in Hong Kong, railed against their government's political processes despite the fear of jail and prosecution. It was known as The Umbrella Movement because they used umbrellas to withstand the pepper spray the police used to disperse the crowds.

An earlier revolution following repression in Romania in the 1980s was also led by the younger generation and the disenfranchised who felt they had nothing to lose but their lives. Theirs was a demonstration of people power. Ceausescu's austerity and tyrannical measures included detaining and investigating anyone suspected of propaganda against the government's economic, cultural and spiritual oppression so it required great fortitude to participate in the uprising. Their strength to withstand harsh authoritarian rulers eventually led to the downfall of the Romanian dictator and his wife.

Stress – a normal physiological reaction – when combined with a predisposition or genetic vulnerability to lack of confidence and anxiety, can be exacerbated when you're pressured by others. Genetics, diet, family and other environmental influences, drugs and cognitive mastery impact on your sense of competence, values and beliefs.

When stressed or anxious, you may be too frightened to say what you really think. The media is complicit in pushing society's ideals and may promulgate the government or businesses' agenda. Isolated from family or support networks during the pandemic, it's little wonder that psychological distress is one of the world's most prevalent mental health disorders among the general adult population.

Your genetics may contribute to your sense of coping and well-being but too many stressors can impact adversely on your mental health, particularly if you have a dearth of strategies or are overwhelmed by the volume of information without time for reflection. If you're increasingly unhappy with aspects of society or frustrated that your efforts make no difference, choose to let go of this negativity, turn away from the media and turn towards nature. See how peaceful you feel? Remember, you've managed effectively on multiple occasions in your life. Be assured that you can and will manage stressors.

Renew your insight and broaden your range of expectations. It's not the time to procrastinate. It's time to be more assertive, open and honest in what you say and do.

Having read this far, you'll now have a clearer picture of who you are and the factors that impact you as you live with the fast-paced challenges of everyday life. You'll be aware of how fragile confidence can be and how self-esteem can be eroded by globalisation, technology, the media, advertisers, peer pressure and the busyness of life.

Can you minimise the conditions that detract from your confidence? Are you ready to address hitherto under-recognised, unreported or unspoken topics that have implications on your well-being? Be empowered through your broadened understanding of where you sit in the modern world.

Chapter Six

We have been addressing factors that contribute to you feeling worthwhile negative but there's more to understand if your life is to be both confident and meaningful. Years of working with clients from all walks of life and at every different life stage have convinced me that we each need to have something or someone beyond ourselves to care for if we're to appreciate and fully embrace a confident life.

It's important that your time is spent meaningfully as you move through the various stages of life. When you engage in hours undertaking work and career, regardless of what it is that you do, the time you give needs to be fulfilling. Similarly, when you create and nurture a family and all that passes in between until finally you arrive at old age, it's important to feel satisfied.

Your life journey may be filled with care and concern about what you can do for others or the more diametrically opposite cult of 21st-century individualism. Perhaps as you observe individuals from politicians to parents and colleagues who put her/himself first, you think that you belong to a society of narcissists. When it comes to those who make the rules, do you feel that you are governed by those who self-sacrifice to support the growth of your community and deserve your loyalty or self-interested politicians? Does your workplace consist of employees and/or colleagues who demonstrate self-centeredness, entitlement and lack of respect or hard-working, caring individuals?

Individualists, being mostly concerned about themselves, don't promulgate loyalty to you or each other. Their shallow behaviour in seeking the temporary satisfaction of every need leaves you bereft of company with whom to share depth and meaning. They model discontent rather than confidence.

Instead of espousing greed and self-interest, accept yourself as part of something greater as your presence makes an impact on the world.

An Authentic, Caring Life

How you think and act in relationships is important if you seek to contribute towards helping build a better future for others. If you're confident, you can assist others to live a more authentic life. Assisting people to achieve their potential, as well as your own, and comforting and supporting others allows you to enjoy simple pleasures. You'll also be attracted to helping occupations, including health, education and law.

As you think about your life and contribution to this world, it's sobering to deliberate on what would you want as an inscription on your tombstone. Your contemplations may have you enquiring what was/is your place in the lives of children and others. Your looks, achievements, occupation, people you know or don't know, places you have been or not, the size of your bank balance, your health or your age won't be relevant in death, but these thoughts prompt you to consider how you might act to ensure a better world for the next generation.

It's important for your contentment that you're authentic in whatever you do now and in the future. This applies to the simplest of things. For example, even the everyday task of eating can be more fascinating once you're not so worried about what, how much and with whom you eat or what others think of your choices. You'll be less interested in hurrying through a meal and more interested in savouring the taste of simple, healthy food if the person(s) in whose company you're eating is being respectful.

You can be more considerate if you're aware of the bigger picture, including the land, the farmer(s), and the effort it took to present your food. This was something Harry had yet to learn.

Harry Explores His Thinking

Having lived in cities his whole life, Harry paid little attention to people's input into his everyday needs. When it came to food, he never stopped to consider what he was ingesting, who was involved or how it was produced. His only concern was to have an enjoyable dining experience unrelated to consideration of the effort made by others, such as the work involved in food preparation and presentation.

At the peak of his working life, everything was smooth sailing for Harry and he was filled with confidence. Until, that is, at the age of 44, when he found himself alone. Having been married for nearly 20 years, this was inexplicable and his world fell apart.

He'd never stopped to think about relationships, other people's feelings, appearances or what he was doing to his body. Triggered by his wife's announcement that she was leaving him, everything he'd known and believed changed. He struggled to understand why she'd left and spent countless hours involved in introspection. Despite this, he could come up with no explanation for the turn his life had taken.

One factor he explored was his image. Having paid it little notice throughout his life, he became concerned about how he came across to others. He thought if he could comprehend that, it would shed some light on why she'd left. But no matter how much he thought about it, he couldn't understand what he'd done or not done that caused her to leave.

He told me he'd always been a hard worker. He put in long hours at work so he could provide financial security for his family and he thought that made him a good husband. He didn't abuse her; he gave her everything she wanted and he asked for nothing in return.

As we talked, over time, he was able to look anew at his previous thinking and past behaviours. Harry acknowledged that, despite his high-powered position as second in charge of a large corporation, he was filled with blame and self-doubt about his abilities in the workplace. He'd been overlooked for promotion to the top position of CEO several times, after which he remembered feeling deflated.

He'd sensed he was doomed to always take second place in his corporate life. He'd reached the position of deputy, but second from the top was demonstrably inadequate for his wife. She was image-conscious and enjoyed her standing in the community based on his position, but when he kept being overlooked, she nagged and belittled him in front of others.

He unpacked his life story. It emerged that he'd been fearful since childhood. He'd been raised in a cold family and received little praise. From our conversations, he finally made the association between his anxiety and fear growing up as the child of an abusive father. He recalled that his father constantly compared him with his brother, reminding him that he'd never be equal to him. Harry felt that whatever he did, it was never good enough.

His mother had tried to compensate for his father's brutish behaviour, but that placed Harry in the awkward position of being teased as a mummy's boy.

From what he recounted, Harry was a skilled manager and projected an outward appearance of confidence to staff and customers. They weren't to know that inwardly he was always second-guessing himself.

He said he'd become used to the notion that his wife and children didn't respect him, only the money he brought home to fund their lavish lifestyles. The busy social whirl they created gave him no joy. He preferred a quiet life with a few close friends. He put every available hour into his work at the expense of his own buried wants and needs. He thought by putting his family's wants first, he would earn their thanks. He couldn't understand what more he could have done to prevent being left alone while his wife moved on.

Harry was stuck. He worried that some deficiency in him had caused the breakup, but no matter which way he reviewed their life, he couldn't comprehend the reason it went wrong. He explained that he'd never wanted to disrupt the children so at the separation, he gave his wife everything. She remained in the house. He relinquished all their investments to her and moved into a small apartment surrounded by few trappings from his former life.

His wife continued her busy social life, financially secure thanks to Harry's generosity.

She had time and energy to manage the family and start a new relationship whereas Harry barely saw his children, having thrown himself even further into work. His self-confidence was at an all-time low.

He transferred the same behaviours from his work environment to his self-development sessions until he recognised that diligence, hard work and conscientious behaviours alone were not enough for the board to appoint him as CEO. Nor were these behaviours alone sufficient in managing his personal development journey. As he uncovered the extent of his faulty thinking, he grasped how it had impacted his feelings and behaviour. Our next step was for him to learn more helpful, healthy ways of thinking and behaving.

Harry worked hard during and between our sessions, coming to terms with the reality that his negative thinking had influenced how he felt, and his actions. He'd been uptight for as long as he could remember, so we introduced relaxation. This helped him stop pushing for answers. He converted to a more mindful approach, dispelled stress, slowed down and appreciated the small things.

Being more honest with himself, Harry realised he'd sabotaged every opportunity to become CEO. Further, he realised that his low self-esteem and his feelings of unworthiness meant he never stood up to anything, including his wife and children. They walked all over him and he allowed himself to listen to them berate him about never achieving the top job. Harry's lack of confidence had allowed others to bypass him, including his wife.

As Harry became more conscious of his previously negative thinking and realised that he had choices, instead of being consumed with worry that he was destined to always be second fiddle, he reframed his thoughts about his role at work. Instead of always wanting more recognition, he decided to consciously embrace the role of deputy. Once he saw it as a positive means of enabling him to let go of the enormities of responsibilities associated with being CEO, he invested more time in interpersonal relationships.

Slowing down instead of feeling lost and no longer spending every waking moment at work, Harry found the time and renewed energy to explore innovative interests. He reconnected with former friends. He found that he was meeting new like-minded people outside work as well.

Through a chance encounter with a fellow while both were waiting for the lift at his apartment, their discussion about politics resulted in Harry accompanying him to a political meeting. Both parents, they held similar views about the government and the resultant devastation of the changes to the economy that would impact their children and future generations. As Harry's interests blossomed, he found confidence talking with others involved in politics and considered joining a political party.

Harry's life turned around. He knew there'd be setbacks as he had a whole life time of negative thinking to release. Newly self-assured, he was adamant that he had the necessary skills. He determined that by making the changes slowly he would not damage his newly developed confidence.

Your Associations

Who do you seek out? Are you like the newly confident Harry or do you associate with people who have confidence, self-assurance and power, whereas you do not ? Is this a mechanism for overcoming fear that you are devoid of these characteristics? Do you think that by being in the same orbit, the personal power and strength of your heroic figure will rub off on you and others will think of you in the same light? This is one way to cover a feeling of inadequacy, yet by surrounding yourself with people you admire maybe you're overlooking your contribution to their lives.

You can't buy genuine affection or admiration although lacking confidence, maybe you're trying to do that. Do you buy gifts, use praise extravagantly, follow the admired person's every move and fawn over them? Putting someone on a pedestal can seem like flattery, but in reality, it distances them from you.

If you've experienced being placed above someone or you have done it because you felt comparatively unworthy, your relationship is not equal.

If you're the one being feted, it can be stressful too. Knowing you're not perfect you nevertheless feel obliged to keep up a pretense when that person attempts to match you to their idealised version. If they perceive you as strong, you can't show normal helplessness in front of them. In creating this inequality, rather than feeling positive about the person's efforts to appreciate you, noticing their overt signs of admiration and ingratiating behaviour leaves you feeling smothered.

If you're an ageing Baby Boomer, it may seem less important to toady up to a workplace contact. Like Harry, if you aren't in a position where you need to build networks to advance your career, you can make choices about who to accept and reject as you move forward.

Ingratiating behaviour at work or in your social circles by people whose lives are wrought by despair and who've covered it by overdoing their generosity and help need to be avoided until they can manage their feelings of inadequacy. Otherwise, you're at risk of being dragged down by them.

Post-Work Opportunities

When your career and work life is winding down or if you have already left it behind, it's common to feel a bit lost or even helpless. This is especially true if you haven't taken the time to plan for new directions or discovering a purpose beyond work. Once the child-rearing years are behind you, followed by cutting back or cutting out work altogether, you have time to refresh or learn new skills. Remember those hobbies you discarded because you were time-poor or things you told yourself you would do if you only had more time?

You've probably heard the expression 'this is not a dress rehearsal'. This is the only life you'll have and you only get one shot at it. Like Harry, it could be time to re-think what you have or to explore new ideas, begin new activities and get out of your comfort zone through travel or relocating.

Socialising seems easier for more confident people, but with a little practice, you can enjoy it regardless of your stage in life and level of self-esteem. Being actively involved is an antidote to the lack of confidence that arises if you no longer have a daily routine of looking after your family or going to work. It may sound difficult to commit to minding grandchildren, look after pets or volunteer as a retiree. Nonetheless, helping is rewarding.

Families rely on each other. If you're a grandparent, you can offer additional support. As your children bear their own children, if you're located close enough geographically to help with grandchildren or the children of nearby nieces and nephews, the experience is truly rewarding.

Babysitting grandchildren can give you a new lease of life. They can also bring added responsibilities at a time of life when you're ready to retire and travel to far-flung regions of the world or simply join the mobile travelling population of grey nomads in Australia. It's important for harmonious relationships that boundaries are established from the outset.

Economic challenges necessitate that both parents of dependent children have to work, but because of the high costs of child-minding facilities, many grandparents are required to become the de-facto babysitters for working families. Grandparents have a positive influence in teaching grandchild(ren) simple tasks. Perhaps their parents are too busy for play, but you can get down on the floor or go outside to engage in their activities or teach them new things. Mastering tasks as mundane as gardening, sweeping up leaves, ironing or washing the car with you can engender their confidence.

Attendance at courses is an easy way for you to socialise. Libraries hold a huge array of courses from creative writing to family history, arts and crafts and computer skills. These activities, in addition to introducing you to new people, allow you to expand your mind. There are also more specific social activities such as groups meeting to play cards or mahjong, and regular book clubs.

Where there is a local University of the Third Age (U3A) even more courses are offered for a small fee. With more time available approaching or having arrived at retirement, you can explore new activities such as kayaking, line dancing, golf, Zumba, Pilates and bush walking.

Like Harry, you can also rekindle old friendships. Technology enables you to reach out and stay in touch using email, and you can also look out for school reunions to reconnect with others from the past. If none yet exist, you can be the organiser who arranges the gatherings. You may turn to the Internet and Facebook to identify people with whom to make contact, but in reading this far, you'll be mindful of what I've already suggested for those needing to decouple from social media.

You can also join travel groups, retirement groups, groups of people with shared interests such as car enthusiasts or other specific hobby groups where participants come together for fun and friendship. Another way to meet new friends is through clubs. Almost every town or suburb has sports clubs such as netball, bowls, football or surf clubs as well as RSL and other organisations. You can seek out like-minded people through Meetup groups or investigate clubs designed for more specific purposes. Groups involved in helping others in your community include Probus, Rotary, The Smith Family, Lions and Red Cross.

Isobel's Volunteering was an Antidote to Loneliness

When I first met Isobel, she was stressed about her work and retirement options. She felt pressured by working for a boss who was significantly younger. She was also angry at her employers, saying they weren't paying her adequately as she was now expected to work additional hours. She said she'd been perfectly happy at work until the appointment of a new woman. She bitterly attributed the changes to the new arrival.

Throughout our sessions, Isobel recognised that her once-confident automatic thinking had left her. She'd become habitually frightened by the many workplace developments and circumstances that she felt ill-equipped to manage. Despite recognising that fear exacerbated her distress symptoms and practising more helpful coping mechanisms for enhancing her self-esteem, by the end of our first session, she remained adamant that her only option was to leave work.

Isobel lived alone. She had few connections beyond work. As we continued to meet, she slowly began to understand the origins behind her feelings of helplessness and sense of unworthiness. She'd held onto many unresolved issues related to her upbringing and relationships with her parents. As her understanding grew, she re-evaluated her interpretation of the complaint she'd made to her union about her pay and conditions. The more we unpacked what had happened, the greater her understanding. She eventually connected her grievance to unresolved anger issues from her youth.

She described feeling an affinity for the union. Then she noted that the reason it had impacted her was because a union official had been the first person in her life who'd really listened to her. She came to the realisation that her aggrieved protest against her employer was manifested because of past hurts that had nothing to do with her workplace. She said she'd always suffered from a lack of confidence, felt unimportant and that she'd been cast into the role of the black sheep in her family.

Isobel had also made some poor relationship choices over the years. Her automatic coping strategy was to leave. She'd left home early and married the first man who'd shown an interest in her as a way to get out from under her parents' roof. Early in the marriage, he'd become abusive. She'd put up with it for many years until finally, she'd gathered the courage to leave him.

Her parents and siblings judged her harshly. They blamed her for the breakdown of her marriage and offered no support. Once she'd left the marriage, she was temporarily homeless. She cut herself off from her siblings because she could no longer bear their judgement. She rallied under the tutelage of her one true friend, sharing a room and finding new employment. Through hard work and determination, she overcame her circumstances.

However, she cut ties with her best and only friend after constant nagging to re-join the dating scene. She wasn't ready to trust. Worried about being hurt, the strategy she'd adopted was to throw herself into working hard. She'd managed to buy a unit and didn't want to jeopardise that for any man. She had no energy left for socialising and, with the exception of her friend, she decided to avoid relationships.

Isobel's efforts at work paid off. She successfully moved up the hierarchy over the years. She had a successful career, the respect of work colleagues, a little left to pay on her mortgage, and if she was bereft of company, she told herself that she didn't mind. But she was angry with herself for her current state of unhappiness.

When her boss pointed out her retirement options, she panicked. She had no plans about what she would do if not in the paid workforce. Realistically exploring her financial options knew she didn't need to continue in the paid workforce indefinitely, but it was difficult for her to see other possibilities even if retirement was fast approaching. The union's suggestion about supporting her to make a claim against her employer gave her a focus.

Isobel was a caring woman, but she had no children upon whom to lavish her warmth and attention, nor a pet. Even though pets were allowed by the body corporate, she didn't feel comfortable having an animal who would have to stay home alone when she was at work. She worried that a little dog in particular would fret if left alone during the day, or worse, that it would disturb her neighbours. Consequently, she came home to emptiness each day after work and as the years passed and neighbours moved, her quiet life was even lonelier.

Once the union official came into her orbit, she felt valued. She listened to his urging and began to feel aggrieved. This coincided with her GP's referral for therapy. We tried a different approach from the advice from the union about fighting her employer. The bitterness was consuming her. Her fragile confidence was shattered by being more than usually alone.

Isobel's experience of abuse, firstly from her parents and even siblings, then her husband, left her sceptical about socialising or joining groups so we looked into her spending time in nature. She also agreed to research volunteering activities. Initially sceptical, she investigated options involving animals. Realising that volunteering required the same serious commitment that she'd shown in the workforce, she was more open to future possibilities.

These activities imbued her with confidence. The better she felt, the less need she had for involvement with the union. Alongside practising stress-management strategies, Isobel explored activities in her community. The more enthusiastic she became, the more her self-confidence grew.

Finally, she decided that even though no claim was settled nor was she yet officially retired, she'd use her genuine concern and understanding, based on her own experiences of being homeless as well as childless, to try her hand with homeless youth.

She started casually as a regular volunteer on weekends. At each meeting with the homeless, her confidence was strengthened. Finally emboldened by her new decision-making strategies as well as confident in her new role and tools to manage her psychological distress in the future, she decided to let go of her complaint through the union altogether. Next, she reconnected with her friend and concluded therapy.

In the following year, when Isobel returned, I saw a different woman. She explained that with her newly found confidence, she'd left full-time work. Her volunteering role had morphed into a part-time paid position where she felt truly valued, and she also had time for other activities. She was blown away by the unexpectedly emotional farewell from colleagues and was still on the best of terms even with the former new arrival and socialised occasionally with several of them.

Retirement was no longer a consideration in her mind. She was too busy in her voluntary work with young people. The role took her into a couple of local schools where she was thrilled to pass on her positive attitude and skills to young people. She was exhilarated by the results, noticing their enhanced confidence as she accompanied them on outings.

Her attitude was markedly different from the woman I'd first encountered. By putting the needs of others first, she forgot her own incapacitating insecurities. Her positive attitude advanced to the point where she was so excited to share her journey that she'd been asked to be an ambassador for older people within the education sector. She had grown a new network by mixing with other helpers, firstly at training programs and later, through her own efforts at socialising.

Isobel even branched into previously untapped areas. Her new best friend introduced her to the Stephanie Alexander Gardening Program. She confessed that she'd never been much of a gardener in the past, but now couldn't wait to see the results of the plantings she and the students made each week. Today's technological world of computers and smartphones was easily understood by the young people she knew. Having grown up with it, they helped Isobel with technology and she helped them to become stronger emotionally. It was a win-win all around.

She was no longer worried about whether or not her work was paid because her contentment came from giving her time and seeing the look on her charges' faces when they felt her support and achieved small measures of success. She'd also been asked out by a fellow volunteer and was eager to see if a relationship would develop.

Remember Isobel and others if you feel uncertain or afraid. Seek support from friends and family rather than trying to battle issue(s) alone. Letting others know what's happening is empowering. Their understanding will help direct your self-care while facing up to and tackling problems. Once you change negative self-talk and no longer feel afraid if you stand up for yourself, you can be proud of the steps you've made and the hurdles you've overcome.

Thinking of others and how you can help is rewarding as Isobel discovered. Volunteers are welcomed by many community organisations. You can offer support at any age. Like Isobel, once you oust hurdles to your confidence and care for others, loneliness is dispelled.

Chapter Seven

We need caring relationships and support from other people. Regardless of who or what, it's important for your confidence and well-being that you form caring, not abusive, relationships. However, the human need for belonging can cause you to settle for someone less than desirable because you become desperate to feel valued.

Strong emotions can temporarily cloud your judgement. Gaslighting, a form of psychological abuse, can also cause victims to question their own sanity or challenge their perceptions and memories. It leaves victims feeling confused and not trusting themselves.

Overwhelmed by passion initially, as relationships progress, they thrive or in the case of abuse, they deteriorate. A toxic relationship can destroy your confidence, especially when you believe you're unworthy. When combined with fears about making mistakes, rejection, financial troubles or potential homelessness, it diminishes your dreams and well-being. Central to the rhetoric about feeling confident, as you age, your self-assurance and the ability to think logically and rationally can be dented.

Your personality type may predispose you to addictive relationships and/or to work. If you aren't in a relationship or are busy day and night, you're filled with tension. If you're in a relationship, but are fearful about being judged, you may be afraid to ask for help if the relationship turns sour. You'll put up with progressively worse behaviour because you feel trapped until a crisis forces you to act . It takes courage to admit the relationship is a failure because it can detract from your self-respect. Suffering from confidence lost in the relationship or from overwork, this pattern is a precursor to anxiety and ill health.

If you've been acting out of fear, remind yourself you don't have to be something you are not to please a partner, a boss or to fit in with friends. Avoid over-thinking if you're in an uncomfortable relationship or situation.

Be decisive. Leave a relationship that isn't working.

Instead of evading judgemental or negative thoughts in case they detract from your confidence and happiness, as you release unhelpful behaviours, you have greater freedom to rebuild your lost confidence and love your unadulterated self. Your self-confidence can be rebuilt as you regain your healthy internal self-esteem. Once again self-respecting and optimistic, you can anticipate dependability, support and reliability from those you love and in whom you place your trust.

Connect with strong, successful, wealthy, happy individuals who are confident enough to speak their minds. Feel comfortable knowing that people in this circle aren't concerned about appearances or control. They respect your right to hold dissimilar views, lack envy and are genuinely happy about your successes. It's infectious.

As you heal, embrace the unfamiliar without undue concern about the outcome. Your confidence isn't hinged on the success or otherwise of relationships, event(s) or circumstances.

Owning up to what you want to change allows you to rectify it. If your past choices have eroded your self-esteem, make a U-turn.

Practise a confidence mindset. Obviously, some things are outside your control but you can change your thinking at any time.

Persevere in the knowledge that valuing yourself helps overcome negativity and self-doubt – the destroyers of confidence. You don't need validation and approval to know if you've been a good partner. Neither you nor anyone else is perfect but it's important to let go when something isn't right. If you don't have a caring personal relationship, you can still connect with some other living being by befriending a bird, dog or cat.

There's no shame in asking for help. Discussing your situation with others provides new insights or different perspectives. People are usually only too willing to assist, especially if they can see how a relationship or other life decision hasn't taken you in a positive direction. You can talk to your doctor, seek a referral to a psychologist, or if you or someone you know is at risk of immediate harm, call for help. In an emergency dial 000.

View rejection in relationships as an opportunity to reevaluate a situation and if a relationship has run its course, walk away with your head held high. In our culture, certain behaviours indicate insecurity or lack of confidence, such as avoiding eye contact and stooping, a sign of poor posture. Note how you usually sit and stand when you're in company. Is it different from when you're alone? Do you stand tall and straight, shoulders back and head held high? As well as making you look taller, it's better for your posture and, in turn, makes you feel more confident.

Even when you're relaxed and confident in your relationships at home and work, they can take an unexpected turn, as happened to Michelle.

Michelle: Challenges to a Lifetime of Confidence

At a women's seminar, guest speaker Michelle provided a glimpse inside the life of an outwardly confident, successful businesswoman. She was well-groomed, smartly dressed and held herself erect, conveying an air of self-assurance. But as is so often the case, all was not as it seemed, as the following revelations encapsulate.

As she outlined her story, Michelle revealed many accomplishments and successes from the rewarding career she'd carved out for herself. She attributed her triumphs to the childhood values instilled in their children by her parents. She provided a brief glimpse into that childhood and her favourite role models, explaining that her parents met after the war, married, then set about creating a simple but healthy life.

Michelle regaled the audience with stories of her parents' courage, about how they attacked and tamed a harsh snake-infested environment and built their first 'hut', a primitive corrugated iron structure where she lived for her first year of life.

Her memories encompassed an inquisitive childhood. She recounted that, after the evening meal, their father encouraged the children's 'play'. This consisted of problem-solving and required mastering various puzzles designed to develop his children's confidence.

Michelle's strong and caring family modelled love, self-belief, resilience over adversity, strong family ideals and the value of hard work. Growing up, she adopted the same values – positive and self-confident – factors she said served her well in business.

It wasn't until she had her own children that Michelle's confidence was shattered. She began finding it increasingly difficult to maintain her outward composure at work and socially because of her teenage son's erratic behaviour at home. She tried to maintain the appearance that she was on top of everything at work, with friends and among her extended family. The only one who saw her looking frazzled was her husband.

Confident as she was in business, Michelle felt lost when it came to dealing with her son's drug addiction. No matter what they did or said, her son compared himself unfavourably to his brother. Caught out by his father for dabbling in drugs, their son blamed an inherited predisposition to addictive behaviours.

Knowing of potentially serious complications and witnessing the negative consequences on his health and self-esteem, Michelle and her husband tried to get him professional help but he would have none of it. As a parent of a substance abuser, she was beset by guilt and exhausted from keeping it secret, fearing the shame. The fact that she couldn't solve this problem ate away at her confidence, spilling into her work and family life.

Michelle questioned her parenting. Had they missed something that happened during the formative years or was it peer pressure that had turned him from a loving, happy boy into a withdrawn young man? She read all she could and worried that if he was enmeshed in a culture based around drug use or other addictions it would be difficult to break free, both from the cravings, compulsions and the dysfunctional lifestyle.

She did courses and educated herself about the complications. Upon learning that addictions are not limited to substances, she worried even more. She learnt that it stemmed from his fears about not being loveable, respected or good enough. He felt a failure.

Michelle's childhood, having been filled with praise and raising her children the same way, she hadn't comprehended the severity of peer pressure. She'd been aware of the effects of peer group pressure arising in the schoolyard but she believed she'd taught her children resilience. Delving into what had happened, Michelle understood that her son had inherited his father's sensitivity. This, coupled with the immense pressure in adolescence to keep up with his peers, was apparently too difficult.

She attributed her son's drug use to his lack of a healthy self-concept and his method of blocking out negative feelings .

She knew they all needed professional help. From her research, Michelle was aware that therapy only worked when the user was ready. She was nervous that their son wasn't ready to accept help, despite the damage caused by his addiction. All she could do was pray.

To help herself, she joined a parent group. Meeting other parents of children with addictive behaviours from gambling to the internet, video gaming, over-work, exercise, shopping and more, was cathartic. She stopped trying to find a reason for what had caused his distress and stopped trying to push him into therapy.

She knew that not every confident child had a similar family. Her husband's parents had not been nurturing. Even so, her confidence, individual beliefs and the values that had hitherto guided her life were challenged by her son's addiction. The parent support group helped restore her healthy self-regard, but what helped the most to restore her confidence was the fact that her son moved out.

Michelle confided in her brother. Hearing about their dilemma, her brother, with whom Michelle's son had a mutually respectful relationship, offered him a position as a jackaroo. It came at just the right time. By then her son was becoming involved with a criminal element. Fortunately, he took the option his uncle offered and moved to the country.

A typical day at the farm consisted of getting up at dawn, drenching sheep, mustering, fixing fences and helping in the kitchen. After all that, he was exhausted. Gradually, his withdrawal symptoms lessened and he found that he loved the rural life. He went from strength to strength, from farmhand to trainee property manager, and turned his life around completely.

He was in awe of his uncle, a no-nonsense man. The whole family felt indebted to him. But the uncle praised their son because, in the end, it was he who made the choices and did the hard work to overcome his demons. Michelle concluded her talk by telling us what she'd learnt from her son and she proudly recounted the news that today her son is a happily married man who was about to become a father.

Her business survived and thrived once she confided in the staff. Because she was honest about why she'd been so down, the staff rallied. She picked herself up. The family settled; she regained her business mojo. As the CEO of a successful business attributed to her hard work and ethical behaviour, Michelle's story represents another confident life.

Like Michelle, is there a relative or someone you remember who had a profound influence on you? Was it positive? Is there someone to whom you felt, and/or currently feel special? Have you felt frustrated, anxious or angry about how others are behaving, as she did?

Maybe you tried drugs or engaged in other addictive behaviours to dull your perceptions, block out feelings of inadequacy or deal with loneliness. Perhaps you've tried to change another person's behaviour, especially if you saw it as self-destructive, and you've been thwarted attempting to redirect them.

Finally, as Michelle did, realise that you can't change anyone else, especially if they don't want to change. All you can change is the way *you* think and how *you* behave.

Factors Impacting on Self-Confidence

There is a myriad of factors at work against developing healthy self-esteem extending across the lifespan, from childhood to mid-life and our senior years, that influence confidence.

Relationships are notoriously challenging and competitive. You may feel criticised because of the school you attended, choices you made for your children's education, your family's marital or financial status, occupation(s), home environment or the physical appearance of yourself and members of the family.

Location

Australians are a beach-loving culture. Warm waters and clear blue skies convey an image of relaxation. Coastal living continues to be popular. Housing has evolved, creating multiple choices for living environments, including options aimed specifically at retirees such as the Baby Boomers who spearheaded sea change and tree change movements.

It's no longer just retirees flocking to the seaside. Southerners have always moved north to embrace the warmth and relaxed lifestyle of the sunshine state. But when their government implemented heavy-handed draconian rules, many more decided to escape. Adults were ordered to remain within a five-kilometre radius of home, children and teens were banned from playgrounds and schools, and punishments were meted out to those who protested against the restrictions. This made many decide to move north to save their mental health.

The necessity to move house, such as because of your partner's work or to help children with special needs, has always been socially challenging. Moving out of your comfort zone can feel lonely, especially when you're in transition or re-settling and your relationships and the circle of people with whom you've shared day-to-day interactions diminishes.

It's difficult to know when to move or downsize, estimate the best market and get out at the right time. No one has the benefit of hindsight before making the move. You may procrastinate for years about these issues as you approach middle age. Unfortunately, many leave it until a situation arises that removes your choice.

Many older people don't want to leave the security of a home where they have a lifetime of memories. It's not unusual, as you move towards older age, for even the most confident person to become fearful of venturing far from the safety of your home, especially if you live alone. Moving house can also be the desire of one but not the other.

Perhaps you've been a keen gardener and are therefore reluctant to leave your home with its gardens to go and live in a unit or apartment. Nevertheless, each step offers you, as a confident person, an opportunity to engage in new goings-on and enjoy new friendships.

Isolation

Until you adjust to a new environment, isolated from former friends, life can be difficult. Removed from your familiar surroundings, it takes time to establish new social connections. You probably feel temporarily insecure. Physical and psychological health complaints are associated with loneliness so you need to work at making new connections to stave off a loss of confidence.

Humans are social animals. We need others in our lives. Technology keeps us indoors where we're less likely to interact with new arrivals in our street. Children who once played outside and through whom adults met each other, are now more likely to be involved in organised sport or other after-school activities away from the home. Upon their return, they probably go indoors and sit in front of a screen.

When children move schools, just as when adults move, they have to put themselves forward if they're to make new friends. Any dent in confidence can be alleviated once you feel connected to your community.

Work Transitions

Workplace transition programmes, appropriate for people normally approaching retirement age, weren't available to the many who lost their jobs during the pandemic. If you were forced into early retirement, you missed the opportunity for the usual gradual transition into the next life phase.

Your fully functioning essence is central to being respected, recognised, esteemed and valued by yourself and others. Without it, psychological health is not possible. Work environments are now more age and health-friendly with functionally designed office spaces. Nevertheless, you may have chosen to leave the work environment or move from a place where you have built up a social network.

Work enhances self-confidence so being forced into part-time or unemployment can negatively influence your self-esteem. Made redundant, losing your job through company restructuring, having to relinquish your job as happened when mandated medical procedures were enforced during the pandemic, you need strategies to make the transition. If you found it too difficult to go from a full-time employee, surrounded by colleagues, to a stay-at-home individual with no support, join those who are choosing on-going work in retirement. This enables you to continue interactions and maintain relationships.

Health and Age

Vast sums of money poured into health by governments is doing little to alleviate the challenges in the health care workforce. It's still a struggle to keep up with the demand for services, especially as we're living longer and in mixed family arrangements.

Despite the advances in food, hygiene and modern medicine, we have high numbers of younger people being diagnosed with autism, heart conditions, stroke, cancer, neurological disorders, body dysmorphia and mental health issues, many of whom still live in the family home. The older we get, the more likely we are to have back and neck pain, hearing loss, cataracts, osteoarthritis, diabetes, depression and dementia, which makes caring for an adult child difficult.

Health, mental and physical, yours, your partners and/or extended family members, will play a part in your decisions now and in the foreseeable future. Although health issues can impact at any age, for a multitude of reasons, it's important to remain alert to good health.

Statistical records compiled by the Australian Institute of Health and Welfare[12] expose the differences between older men and women when it comes to illness and the leading causes of death. Both share chronic conditions including arthritis, asthma, back pain and problems, cancer and cardiovascular disease, but for men, coronary heart disease – a leading cause of death – is becoming more prevalent across all age groups. Among women aged 65–74, the leading cause was lung cancer but in older age groups, it's dementia, including Alzheimer's disease.

To be confident whatever your age, requires a realistic assessment of your health needs. If you're older or have an impairment, are you at risk of falling or unable to fully maintain your current home because of its size or the garden areas? Are you losing mobility due to skeletal deterioration? Just because you're currently healthy doesn't mean you can escape the reality that everyone deteriorates. Your bones and muscle mass change, as do your teeth and hair, even if you maintain an unchanged exterior through some enhancement procedures.

Regardless of your health, if your partner's health deteriorates, it can limit your lifestyle choices. Clearly, there will be risks if you or a partner is disabled or you notice little signs that one of you is becoming frailer or less cognitively competent as each birthday passes. S/he may lose their vision, hearing or memory. You may be with a partner who has special needs.

Negative thoughts about ageing or dealing with illness, recognising you're unable to do the same things physically that you did beforehand, and awareness of changes in your appearance can leave you feeling insecure and compound low self-regard. Notwithstanding the sorrow of such losses, you can reflect confidently on the pleasures you still have.

Advertisers, health professionals and governments are introducing more targeted services knowing that lifestyle, values and needs impact confidence in ageing. Businesses too are making efforts to provide systems and support to manage ageism. As society adapts to a longer age-span and an emphasis on fitness, developers are making special provisions for age-related housing estates. Apartment dwelling is on the rise, especially among retirees for whom over 50s lifestyle estates, gated communities and retirement villages have been designed.

Travel, an option through work or leisure and to help broaden your perspective may not suit both partners at the same time. Your view may differ from your partner, who sees the lack of constraints from work or family commitments as an opportunity to travel or move to far-flung destinations. Many older Australians are continuously on the high seas. Cruise ships provide a suite of activities and adventures, as well as the opportunity to enjoy conversation and good company with peers and others from elsewhere on the planet.

Being with other like-minded people can enhance your confidence. Joining one's peers, including in purpose-designed villages, is beneficial. They're specifically built to incorporate age-related health and fitness facilities, with close proximity to shopping centres, cafes, health care facilities, sporting, artistic and other club activities.

Where do you want to live for the next stage in your life's journey once you leave work?

And with whom? What are your expectations regarding health? If you or your loved ones are advancing to a significantly older age, there are still many aspects of life to be enjoyed. Theatre buffs can still enjoy plays, concerts and movies.

Independence

When everything is going well, you don't necessarily want to think about next year, much less beyond that, or how you'll look or support yourself as you age. Maybe you have a false sense of immortality. However, if you can be sure of one thing it's that no one lives forever. The question of where to live for the longer term and beyond becomes important as you're no longer raising a family and not tied to a work environment.

Once the Family Law Act changed in 1975, the only grounds necessary for divorce became irretrievable breakdown, making property settlements and arrangements for children more straightforward. Changes to the divorce laws mean that instead of remaining in abusive or controlling relationships, women can separate. Maybe you wish to remain in the same location if it's still affordable, or you plan to move into something to better suits your changing needs.

Remaining independent means different things to different people. For one partner, it can be a more vital consideration than the other and depends on a variety of factors, especially uncertainty, anxiety and self-confidence. Downsizing is a decision most couples and families discuss at a stage of life when the children leave home, your parents age or your retirement looms.

Disability

Neither age, disability nor infirmity equate to less mental acuity. It's important to be respectful of each person's wishes regardless of your age and stage of life. Many a confident disabled or older person has travelled to even the remotest places on the planet. Of course, for a disabled or elderly traveller, there can be many challenges, but these can be overcome in the planning stage. If you're involved in the travel process you will recognise if your elderly or disabled person has the same feelings, wishes, dreams and aspirations as a more able-bodied person. Travelling can empower you if embraced with a positive approach.

If you're lucky enough to have a loving partner, their physical presence can be especially comforting during times of indecision or change. In situations where you have to provide additional care for a partner or aged parent, may you find new joy and a sense of meaning as you accept revised circumstances.

Maybe your parents or grandparents have shared stories or you've seen movies in which no matter the age, partners comforted each other through simple gestures such as holding hands, a habit they continued throughout their lives.

Even when outings are limited by age or circumstances, no matter your age, you can wander around a garden or reach for each other across the sofa while watching television. It's soothing to lie in each other's arms and drift off to sleep even at an advanced age or stage of poor health. Many loved ones keep their elderly close, sharing precious memories and touch until they pass away.

Mobility is important to confidence. Yet even if you're prone to falling, as well as the physical implications, being confined to a wheelchair can impact your well-being. Being in a wheelchair is associated with a loss of physical strength. Armed with this knowledge, it's important to maintain your strength, your capacity to earn an income or have some means of financial support, your ability to maintain a home and garden, even driving and being able to go shopping independently.

Simple routines such as going to the bathroom, a task many of us take for granted in our younger years, can be problematic as we age or if we're infirm. It's vital for your confidence that you be allowed to continue to look after yourself as long as possible and this is consistent with living in your own home. Independent living enables you to maintain friendships, enjoy games and sports, share as you choose with neighbours or visitors, have your pets and retain as much privacy as you wish. But like Jean, moving presents a dilemma that could undermine your confidence.

Are you at a point of considering if you really need or want to move? Maybe you're thinking of ways to make your home more user/age-friendly as your needs change. Living in their large family home after retirement, these questions plagued the usually optimistic Jean as she discussed the situation with her husband.

Jean: To Move or Not?

Jean's husband had become very involved as a silent partner with a friend in an online business but many of the people whose company they'd enjoyed, now retired, were constantly travelling the world or cruising. Friends who'd moved into apartments and over 50s villages kept advising Jean to do the same, espousing the freedom that came from no garden or pool to worry about as they simply locked the door and walked away for holidays.

Jean's children also nagged her about moving. Her daughter had moved from their home in an inner-city suburb in Melbourne, with Jean in close proximity, to Victoria's Mornington Peninsula. They wanted Jean to live close to them again, but Jean was worried about following them.

Although her husband, knowing she wanted to remain geographically close to her daughter and grandchildren, agreed about moving, Jean was undecided. They had a companionable group of friends near their old home with whom they shared many social outings. The doctors, chemist, hairdresser and other services and shops were equally familiar and convenient. Moving meant they would be too far away to continue regular socialising within that circle and the stress of being forced to decide caused Jean sleeplessness nights.

She was confused and conflicted about whether to leave her house and the neighbourhood where she was comfortable or to move house to continue to be near her family. She worried how, if they moved location to where she knew only family, she could start over again. Growing up with other children and families in the area where their own children went to school, in the past Jean had easily come to know and befriend people locally. Being older now, she felt as they had no children at home, it would be difficult to break into a new social group.

She was apprehensive that in a new area where she knew no one and was without the icebreaker of children, she would become too dependent on her husband for company. As much as she wanted to be near her children and grandchildren, she was aware that they had their own family needs to consider and she didn't want to intrude or become dependent on them.

Finally convinced by her husband, they sold their home. They made impassioned goodbyes to their friends, all of whom promised to visit. As luck would have it, they found a new house to purchase in an estate in the same neighbourhood as their daughter and her family. Decision made, Jean threw herself into moving.

When next we caught up, Jean had lost that worried look. She explained that as they'd moved into a smaller home, she found it gave her so many more options than she'd expected. Apart from the nearness to her family, the smaller garden was less onerous, and being newer, the house required less maintenance. They felt more inclined to shut the door and go on holidays as their friends had suggested, and in fact by joining them, Jean found they had wonderful catchups with no limitations because they were all away from all their responsibilities.

Jean's biggest change was joining a golf club. Her husband had always played golf, and so as part of her new life, she decided to take lessons. This was the beginning of a whole new interest and she soon became a familiar face in an increasingly social network.

Older Relatives

If you are semi or fully retired, without work routines, there's greater freedom to spend time doing things you want to do and doing things differently. Staying healthy is important, especially if you're taking on extra roles, such as child care or caring for elderly relatives. Jean and her husband continued their independent living but in considering the move, they were aware that there was an over-50s lifestyle village nearby that they could join in the future if their needs changed.

Maybe you have to make decisions about changed living arrangements for yourself or older or impaired relations. It's difficult enough to make emotional decisions about yourself when it comes to moving out of home, but when you're the one who has to make decisions for or on behalf of relatives it can be equally challenging.

If the aged person is unwell or becoming incapable of self-care, it can add an additional burden to even the most compassionate of us.

If you have to place a loved one in a hospital, you may become frustrated by the efforts of staff. No one will look after your loved one as you could. Once you're caught recognising that their care is beyond your ability to manage, it's a very distressing dilemma to face. Battling to negotiate the social services system for the disabled can be fraught with difficulties especially if you're not naturally a confident person.

Accessing the National Disability Insurance Scheme (NDIS) to achieve better care requires tenacity to manage the requisite paperwork that goes into setting up a participant's plan. People with disabilities have complex needs and whilst allocated a budget and plan for their care, provided by NDIS, there are numerous third-party businesses and organisations with whom to interact. It can be daunting for even the most confident of us but is made more difficult when disabled.

You may be the only family member available to make the decisions and to help navigate the complexities of the system, with families spread out across the country and the world. By helping the person with special needs so they don't fall through the cracks or become overwhelmed, your assistance enables them to feel heard and valued. It's important for everyone to feel cared for at every age and stage if we're to remain confident in our ability to do what is right.

Are you the one nominated (or left) to make preparations for any arrangements that will enable your elderly relative to be cared for or nursed as they remain in their own home? Has it fallen on your shoulders to help select entry and facilitate someone's transition into an aged-care facility? It's more difficult if your loved one is disabled by the inability to do something as necessary as swallowing yet is very resistant to moving into a care facility.

For the older age group, there is the Aged Care Assessment Team to arrange the linking of services for an elderly relative. Keeping him or her at home and arranging care through the various aged-care support agencies may be a better option as, at the end of the day, the feeling that you have some control over your life is what gives you confidence. This is true for all of us.

Even if your elderly relative or partner collapses through frailty and illness, being in one's own home and bed can make a world of difference emotionally. If their life is coming to an end, knowing you have done your best for your loved ones will help you feel confident about any decisions you had to make. Be confident that you can and have accomplished what you set out to do with their best interests at the heart of any decisions.

Reflecting on Your Values

Globalisation and changing technologies add another complication. After reading this far, are you concerned that you'll be overwhelmed, unable to keep up with all the changes now and ahead in the 21st century? What is important to you now? Do worries about health, relationships or ageing hold you back?

Have you compromised your values because of fear that you're unworthy? Are you reluctant to say what you think in case others disagree? Are you consciously aware of how your life experiences have shaped your values? Have you been living under the influence of values you've absorbed subconsciously from your childhood?

The following activity will help you identify your thinking:

- Pay attention to yourself as you are right now. Where do you see yourself realistically physically, spiritually, emotionally or intellectually?

- What values are important to you?
- How do they or have they influence(d) your behaviour?
- Have you been living as your fictional self, held back by trying to meet everyone else's expectations, or do you understand what motivates you and applaud your unique individual potential?
- How confident are you that you can chart the rest of your life confidently?

Well done!

Chapter Eight

Having read this far and doing the exercises and/or journalling, you're probably aware of any habitual behaviours that have been holding you back. You'll understand some of the reasons behind your past actions and how managing appropriately is relevant to your confidence.

You know you can't control your life perfectly but you can look favourably on your efforts. You know that if you failed someone or something, it's now in the past. As a normal, fallible human, you can't control every outcome, only do your best with the information you have at the time. Even if what you did in the past wasn't always desirable, what matters is that you can forgive yourself, knowing that you'd act differently if the same situation arose again.

As well as forgiving yourself, you can also forgive others who may have unintentionally or deliberately hurt you. It's more challenging to forgive someone who intentionally harmed you, but the alternative is to be consumed by bitterness and it won't alter the outcome.

Forgiveness enhances contentment. Be satisfied with yourself exactly as you are. Anything less drains your confidence and risks depriving you of the attention and energy that could be used to boost your enjoyment of life.

As you apply this thinking to your body, recognise any personal costs of trying to achieve what doesn't come naturally in order to measure up to some impossible ideal. Genetics, choices, events and opportunities create the reality of your body structure and fitness level today.

Your confidence about your appearance blossoms with compliments about your external appearance. It manifests in the way you hold yourself and how you speak about yourself and others. Being imbued with your own inner confidence, it's easy to find the positives in other people and offer them genuine compliments but make sure to be sincere. You can brighten someone's day with an act as simple as a smile.

As a confident adult, knowing value and transmitting this to other generations is important. If you're a parent or grandparent then you are also a teacher as you impart skills to children and grandchildren. Teachers know that by instructing others, you also reinforce your own learning. You're also a child so let your parent(s) know that you value all they've done for you. It takes no effort and their (surprised) response is ample reward. Pleasure, yours and/or theirs, and respect in all your relationships signifies empowerment.

The lifestyle you lead can be as simple or as complex as you wish. Maybe you worry about the big issues of our time, such as the economy, poverty, drugs or career options. You may prefer a simpler life based on the love and enjoyment of the people in it.

Unwritten Rules

Being involved with a healthy, supportive community underpins confidence. It's important to your well-being that you find contentment, rather than feel unworthy underneath, like you're constantly striving for the impossible. You don't have to win at everything or be the most brilliant in order to fit in.

The particular rules you apply may be so ingrained that you've forgotten why you made those choices about who you mix with or the image you work so hard to portray. Maybe you were previously unaware of the rules you applied subconsciously to yourself about the face you felt you had to present.

Certain unwritten rules can become so ingrained that you habitually behave in certain ways with little awareness or thought. These rules govern your unconscious thinking about the way you're supposed to live and how to earn other people's respect.

If you've never stopped to take the time to explore these 'rules' you may not be aware of how they've impacted you and the times you gained or lost your confidence. Think back over your life to elucidate responses to the following questions. You may discover aspects that could enhance your self-esteem and build even more on your inner confidence. You're not answerable to anyone else and there are no right or wrong answers, so with openness and honesty, consider the following:

- I am happiest when …
- I am good at …
- I think my body is …
- When someone compliments me, I …
- When someone criticises me, I …
- If someone treats me badly, I …

- What keeps me going is …
- When I look into my future, I see …

If you've been busy following habitual rules, you may have avoided or missed opportunities for active and meaningful involvement with family, friends and the unexpected. In the hurry to achieve or if you've settled for make-do rather than taking time out for yourself, you may have bypassed passions for a pallid existence.

Sometimes the joys in life slip away, piece by tiny piece and you don't even notice as you rush to keep up with the unwritten, idealised behaviour you have ascribed to yourself. Can you recall the days when your life was filled with passion and each day seemed so exciting?

Living a mature life can look as if it's more complicated in these multifaceted times. Today's babies and children won't know a world before AI and you're only just coming to grips with it. The environment is more complex, so it may feel easier to retreat to your old rules because you're not sure of your role with the implications of living with AI.

Rules Created by Others

In this era, you can't avoid using computers. They're a necessary tool in the workplace and/or for social connectivity but they come with operational rules. In this case, the government and tech giants are the ones creating them.

But governments have lost our trust. Their campaigns to persuade us to adhere to various rules have to be more and more graphic to draw our attention, such as when trying to ensure we understand the perils of smoking and/or illegal drugs. Despite their best efforts, we have a worse drug problem than ever – vaping has replaced smoking for many and now they've made more rules around that.

Are you waiting for the next edict from the government to tell you how to live life? During the pandemic, people were impacted by difficulties obtaining the basics of adequate food. In housing commission apartments in Victoria, food had to be brought in but subsequently, as reported in *The Guardian* online, the Victorian government had to pay out following a class action from residents who said they were wrongly detained during the pandemic. Collectively, they maintained their right to appeal against the authoritarian behaviour thrust upon them. Upon investigating the matter, the Ombudsman declared 'Some people were without food and medicines. At the tower at 33 Alfred St, the focus of the investigation, residents waited more than a week to be allowed outside under supervision for fresh air.'

Sometimes if your inner confidence is weak, it can be easier to be strong by acting with others. However, when operating as a group, you have to be careful about the motivations of others. Everyone has different rules about how to live life and there's the potential for exploitation if actions backfire due to malicious intent.

In the current harsh economic times, the cost of certain foods is prohibitive but the rules around transport, wages and other costs have resulted in farmers having to bin some of their produce. Meanwhile, you have to pay more.

We have at least a two-speed economy. The purchasing power of members of the generation who became adults at the turn of the millennium – today's young tech millionaires and billionaires – enables them to acquire goods and property at exorbitant prices. Together with overseas competitors, this drives up costs in the housing market and locks out those at the other end of the scale.

The costs of building are constantly increasing. The fact that building materials are now largely obtained offshore impacts reliability and cost. Rental properties are in short supply, partly because the number of migrants accepted into our country outweighs the number of available dwellings. Other factors include increases in landlord's costs, which they then pass on, resulting in some families being unable to afford rent.

A scarcity of housing to accommodate immigrants, refugees and the homeless is not solved by imposing yet another impost on taxpayers. On the contrary, the government is lowering multiple generations of workers' confidence in the Australian dream of home ownership. Despite living in a first-world country, these prohibitive factors impact basic health and housing.

As you reflect on the place of rules within your life, are you aware of what they mean for you? Have you settled for comfort and ease with digital habits such as settling for fast entertainment and instant communication? Thinking about the demands of others or those rules you've created and put on yourself, it may be time to put the brakes on.

As you sit quietly, listen to that tape playing in your head and hear the messages (rules) you've created. Even if you weren't aware of this until now, think about how your actions have been validated or impeded by rules. If unconscious rules have held you back, now is the time to break free from worry. This may require expanding your face-to-face activities and broadening your networks.

Basic Needs: Maslow's Hierarchy

An understanding of psychologist Abraham Maslow's hierarchy of needs[13] enables you to locate the impact and your place according to the five motivations he identified. He described them in the form of a hierarchical pyramid arranged into five categories. In this theory, once a category is fulfilled, we move on to the next level.

In looking into Maslow's hierarchy of needs, you can uncover the five commonalities required by all of us to survive and thrive confidently.

One: Physiological Needs

At the base of the pyramid are physiological needs, the most essential of our needs, including concrete needs such as food, water and sleep. For healthy development, you need food that nourishes your body, a roof over your head to protect you from the elements and adequate rest. You also need adequate finances to purchase the necessities for survival. In Maslow's terms, young people and those unable to compete in the homebuyers' market due to extortionate costs are disadvantaged and unable to attain basic security.

Two: Safety Needs

You need security and a safe environment. This entails feeling safe at work, at home and in the broader environment. It's important for allaying fear and anxiety. Fortunately, living in a developed nation, you're less likely to have these needs impacted unless in an emergency. However, as worry about terrorist attacks and record inflation together with the internet explosion create fear among an entire population, it can drive people to postpone marriage. It can also result in generations continuing to live with parents to save on costs even if they have a prestigious, highly paid professional career, but multiple generational conflicts can lead to impatience.

Three: Love and Belonging

When your basic needs for survival are met, you focus on the next level. You need friendship, love and to experience belonging. You need to feel loved and also give love to others.

Feeling loved and accepted includes both romantic relationships as well as belonging to family, the social world and community. Many researchers have subsequently explored the importance of social connectivity for physical health, and the negative consequences of unmet needs and isolation on health and well-being.

Four: Esteem Needs

The fourth component is self-esteem and confidence. It involves feeling good about yourself. Self-confidence is also associated with having your achievements and contributions valued by others. When that happens, you're likely to feel important.

However, with technology integral to everyone's daily life and decreasing face-to-face communication, you can become fixated on personal feedback for a sense of self-worth. As wide-spread mental health problems explode, impacting on security and self-esteem, it's incumbent on parents, teachers and bosses to help younger generations develop a realistic sense of self-worth to build true and lasting confidence.

Whether it's searching for something to purchase, job hunting, learning options, travel, business development, networking or entertainment, if you're from an older cohort, you'll recognise that, as well as the speed of communication, the young today live in an era where every child receives a prize. Even the one who comes last gets an award for participation, leading to a sense of entitlement regardless of lack of experience. These factors shape confidence.

Some of the first four categories overlap or only partly meet your needs at the time. It's not definitive that you experience each level before moving to the next. For example, when you have a meal with others, you're meeting your physiological need for food, but you're also satisfying the need associated with feeling a sense of belonging. Or if you work as a paid carer, this might satisfy your need for a wage, which enables you to be fed and sheltered but also fulfils your need to feel a sense of social connectedness and esteem as you feel good about helping.

Five: Self-actualisation

The final category, self-actualisation or self-fulfilment, is harder to reach and will look different for everyone. It may be that you achieve it by helping others or through your achievements. Essentially, it's about feeling that you're doing what you were meant to do and experiencing a heightened sense of fulfilment and motivation by realising your fullest potential.

Once these aspects are in place, you're positioned for inner confidence whatever your accomplishments. According to Maslow, you can then achieve self-actualisation, by which he meant what can be accomplished when you fulfil your potential. These are worthy goals to experience at any stage of life.

When assessing Maslow's hierarchy of needs, remember how quickly families, colleagues, peers and communities banded together when told of a potential health threat from COVID-19. People united around a common threat, but friendships and the very family to which one belonged were often the same one that turned on any member who failed to conform, such as the nurses, teachers and front-line workers who were stood down and were denigrated, isolated and/or lost their jobs. To regain their sense of belonging, they formed new groups with others who'd similarly questioned the authorities' decisions.

We all want to belong and although we can't all agree, security arises from being with others who share our values. The children of our ancestors, devoid of television and other electronic devices, supported each other in friendship. They learnt self-reliance, played unsupervised outdoors in all weather, climbed trees and learnt first-hand about risks, relying on each other and their imaginations.

Confidence Today

Do you catch yourself living in the past, daydreaming about bygone times when you were confident about the place of everyone and everything in your world? Do you recognise and deal with your fears by trying to be someone other than who you are? Is your appearance the only thing you focus on in the here and now? You may find yourself at an age when you want birthdays to stop.

Ageing is normal. Inner confidence is not. Even if you're genetically fortunate to be positively programmed, depending on your life's influences, it can be pierced and take some work to restore. Despite all today's advancements, levels of confidence in the community generally are at an all-time low.

The advent of television and its imagery beamed into living rooms, together with reporting of negative predatory adult interactions with innocent children induces fear and a loss of trust among families. This fear sees generations of children constantly monitored by cautious adults. They keep children indoors where television and technology have largely replaced reading. And yet it's not the environment outside the home that's so dangerous. Evidence from domestic violence studies shows that much of the abuse occurs within the family unit, a place where you expect to belong and feel safe.

Traditionally, your 20s to 30s is the time when you settle for a loving relationship. Maybe a friendship grows and you marry. You plan a future together, take on responsibilities in the workplace, plan a home and begin a family. In Maslow's terms, you enjoy the feeling of belonging that comes from being in a secure relationship.

Brides look so happy on their special day. Your grandmothers probably had little access to the trappings of the beauty industry but glowed with love. To enhance their confidence, modern brides spend extraordinary amounts on treatments and products to enhance their appearance on their special day. But despite the industry devoted to making a wedding special, it's still the inner beauty and the radiant glow when in love that truly makes a bride beautiful.

Brides commonly suffer from nerves about the day, so it takes great courage to withstand the pressures to spend exorbitant amounts for one event, but being in love and knowing someone finds you beautiful gives you an inner confidence.

We're all vulnerable to some degree according to the attention paid to us by others. How do you perceive yourself as you look at your image on screen, when you look in the mirror or when you engage in conversations with strangers vs friends? Is it different when

reflected in the eyes of someone who cares about you? Do you diminish positive responses from family and friends? Do you pay more attention to comments by the person who treats you critically and then become consumed with worry about what they think?

Never Too Old

As a younger person, your skin was elastic skin not wrinkled and your body was minus the effects of gravity, which pulls everything lower. Nevertheless, with a confident approach to life, you'll be happy in your skin and content with your life at whatever stage you've reached in your journey thus far.

Imagine yourself already beautiful, competent and a loving friend. Reassess your values and how you want to spend the rest of your life, being prepared to change any old dysfunctional or ingrained habitual behaviours. Understand and celebrate the changes that arise with ageing, and compliment yourself for knowing you've survived and created the life you've lived.

As you age, you're free from the old societal beliefs, such as 'I must have enough money then I will be happy' or 'if only I work harder then I will feel secure'. Feelings turned inward can become toxic and/or fill you with anxiety and fear. Your main responsibility as you age is for your own well-being. It can be easy to self-sabotage a new behaviour when you've lived so long being negative, but you can learn new ways.

Notice how your mood improves when you enjoy being your age. Age gracefully and trust yourself to let go of illusive, habitual thoughts and absorb Shane Gould's advice.

Shane Gould won *Australian Survivor* in October 2018. She was a world-famous swimmer, winning five gold medals in the 1972 Olympic Games. Now she's the oldest competitor to win against contenders half her age. 'People shouldn't underestimate what a 60-year-old can do!' she said.

Her message to over-60s is that it's never too late and being older doesn't equate to being washed up. She used her win to highlight that despite social pressures that push older people to the side, everyone, particularly women, is encouraged to assert themselves. Her message is not to accept that being older means you're disposable. You have too much wisdom and experience. She says you have to fight to continue to contribute and participate in society.

Some people will be prone to osteoarthritis or other conditions particularly associated with ageing. For people whose work is more physical and for all of us as we age, our manual dexterity deteriorates. If one gene is damaged, we're usually able to apply another gene to fill in, until the day that too many joints are damaged or too many arteries calcify and we can't wear down any further.

However, a longer life can present you with multiple and rich opportunities. You may have more time to spend with loved ones, for family , the community and to engage in hobbies. Some health and education professionals who lost their jobs due to the COVID-19 mandates have subsequently re-trained and found new fulfilling careers. Why not consider pursuing career prospects in an area that is new to you or that has only recently been developed?

Strategies

New habits can be learned and change is inevitable.

Technology Downtime

Technology is here to stay. However, confidence can be boosted or dashed based on something as artificial as the number of likes to a story you made for social media, or the reactions of others to a story you posted on Facebook. Thinking outside the box or on in-depth face-to-face communications is replaced with ingesting imagery and content that has been created for you.

You may feel that you belong to a certain group or have a special connection with a person you've seen on the screen. The explosion in social media allows you to feel connected but removes the physical face-to-face personal context. You can spend hours mutely watching or reacting to images on a screen, perhaps as a way to unwind after a busy day.

Try to spend time without your iPhone and iPad. Instead, metaphorically (or literally) lie back on the grass watching clouds and thinking creatively. Note the difference it makes to your mood, creativity and relationships.

Pets

Ill health or a relationship breakdown can challenge your security and dreams for the future. Seeing your plans and the loss of all you'd taken for granted fade due to loss of health or a loved one induces concern in even the most confident person, then your energy is depleted.

Being loved by a pet can fill that void when you're missing friends or lacking the support from being in a loving relationship. Animals are non-judgemental. Tending pets and even wild birds provides a renewed sense of purpose as you're responsible for someone or thing other than yourself.

Stand Up for Yourself

If you've been hurt, change any negative self-talk, let go of fear, purge yourself of unnecessary baggage and take steps to nurture yourself. Learn to trust again, be open to new friendships, renew old connections and even find a new love interest.

The beauty industry and those destroyers of self-esteem who seek to propagandise us into their ways of behaving can't come between true friends or people in love if you don't spend your life worrying about what you look like. Make the most of life regardless of loneliness, ill-health or ageing.

A smile goes a long way and costs nothing. Respect the rights of others whilst feeling free to express your own feelings. Don't expect to always get your own way but don't waste energy holding onto negative or aggressive feelings. Whatever your age and stage of life, ditch self-limiting beliefs that have you burying your feelings because you're frightened to express yourself.

Realistic Self-talk

In January 2021, in an article published in *The Lancet* entitled 'Healthy Ageing for a Healthy Planet'[14], the authors reported that world-ide in 2018 for the first time in history, we had more people over the age of 65 than children younger than five years of age. In 2019, the United Nations' World Population Prospects report projected that by 2030, the number of people aged 60 and over will rise by 38% globally. The UN also warned that, with the longer life spans, some countries may not be adequately prepared.

Apply Shane Gould's rationale to your body and you're ready as you age. Check in with yourself. What are your messages to self about ageing whether it's yourself or a loved one? What are you doing to compensate for losing muscle mass?

Resistance Training

No matter how old you are, you can still build muscle and improve your health through resistance training. Studies have even shown that you can gain strength in your 70s and 80s.[15]

Maybe you or an aged relative are suffering from muscle atrophy due to malnutrition, genetics, lack of physical activity or a medical condition. Let your doctor refer you to a physiotherapist for resistance training involving weights, specialist machines, and using your own body or resistance bands. You only need to do it two or three times a week – the muscles need time to recover in between sessions.

Walking

Value exercise and activate your cardiovascular system to maintain physical health. Walking at a reasonable pace and intensity to increase the demands on your heart, lungs and muscles is an excellent and free activity. It's also social. You can walk with a friend or in a group. Walking heart healthy groups can be found, or runs held by most local councils at no cost, or for a minimal donation.

Physical Activities

Councils also have a multitude of physical activities to keep you from becoming too sedentary. From the more strenuous Pilates, canoeing, aerobic and strength-building activities, to gentle tai chi, chair yoga and balance classes, there's sure to be something to suit your level of fitness. Attending community classes has the bonus of keeping you in touch with other people at a similar age and stage of life if the gym is not for you.

Maybe you prefer aqua classes at a heated pool or joining a group of regular swimmers for an early morning beach dip or walk. Ballroom dancing requires dedication but at any stage of fitness, you can easily join line dancing classes if they're available in your area. Tennis and table tennis, golf and archery are just some of the many activities to help you get out and about, which contributes to your confidence.

Social Activity

If you prefer card or board games, you may find a mahjong group or bridge club. For the artistically minded there are classes in all mediums. Sports clubs are always grateful for any help you can offer, even if your contact-sport-playing days are behind you. Check out the activities near you.

Fun

It's joyful to live longer if you're happy and content within yourself. You can enjoy a wardrobe filled with clothes that are comfortable without concern that the items are no longer fashionable. Fashions are cyclical, so your existing wardrobe, filled with clothes pushed to the back because you thought they were out of fashion, can be brought out for a second airing.

Secondhand clothes shopping is popular as a new trend. If you're attending a special function or themed party, it can be fun to use your imagination to buy something pre-loved or new. When you're not restricted, why not try new styles? A confident woman or man, not beholden to any fashion trend, you can wear what you want with assurance and poise.

Red Hats and Ageing 'Disgracefully'

Maybe you've noticed a group of women wearing outrageously large, elegant red hats on their heads, atop dresses in the darkest of purples. If you're inquisitive, they will be very welcoming and pleased to explain their attire.

This group of women challenge ageing and the doyens of fashion by wearing obviously over-the-top ill-matching colourful apparel. They're members of the Red Hat Society, a worldwide movement whose intention is to promote confidence among women. They obviously enjoy being together and having fun and will confess that they're quite comfortable frequently and freely expressing their point of difference.

Aware that purple and red don't match, nevertheless they define themselves fearlessly by wearing purple clothing donned by garish red hats. The under-50s wear mauve attire and pink hats. You often see these groups, characterised by their gaudy dresses and hats, out to lunch. This appalling fashion attracts attention but undeterred, these women celebrate life to the fullest as part of a world-wide movement.

You don't have to wear a purple or red hat to enjoy life. Your resilience, optimism and self-awareness of your choices, both from the past and onwards, have incrementally developed your character. Don't give your power away.

Like the Red Hat ladies, harness your personal power to project inner beauty, regardless of fashion and trends at any age. Sure, your hair turns grey when it runs out of pigment, but you can add colour artificially. If you elect to have laser surfacing treatments to rejuvenate your skin, go for it. Worried that your memory, judgement, planning and processing speeds have been generally declining, view things in a positive light.

Not worrying when people point out your imperfections is healthy. Age spots on the skin can be seen as mechanisms for clearing out waste. There's no right and wrong way to age. When you catch yourself noticing residual unhelpful memories, confront the demons that attack your confidence by channelling the Red Hats.

Don't overthink. Your life and your thoughts are too important to be drowned under commercial interests or distortion and coercion by the media or your peers. Rid yourself of any subversive negative messages, remembering that fulfilment comes from the inside out. Be conscious not to settle for choices based on fear.

Claim your independence rather than being condemned to fitting in. Be unique, a brave individual, true to yourself and unashamed of difference. Even if you can't put it into words or join a Red Hat ladies' group, feel satisfied that you have a body that functions exactly as it was designed to and you're deserving of a healthy life.

As you age, growing confident and strong, fill your life with meaning, devoid of restraint by unwritten rules. Happily share your life with colleagues, friends and family, whilst remaining true to your own values and integrity.

Chapter Nine

Maintaining the confidence to express your views is difficult when, manipulated daily by external forces, you are fearful. Anyone's confidence can be eroded by a constant barrage of doomsday propaganda cleverly interwoven into mainstream society.

Fear is such a powerful force that it can be difficult to maintain your confidence when an alternative narrative is presented by trusted sources. It's hard to hold different points of view or stand your ground against fashions and trends promulgated by the media or your peers. It takes a strong will to see through advertising and all the many forms of propaganda.

Many young and older men and women in schools, universities, workplaces, and at family and social gatherings stay silent, fearing they'll be muzzled if their views differ from colleagues, friends, family or mainstream media. The terms misinformation and disinformation are a disincentive, especially for those speaking out against prominent issues.

However, some have always been courageous enough to speak regardless of holding divergent views. The differences between the sexes in the 20th century, when women did what was expected of them, were turned on their head by the feminist movement of the '70s. It gave women a voice and resulted in legislative changes including federally funded childcare. The women grew confident about fashions, roles and the right to be heard.

In *The Female Eunuch*[16], a text important to the feminist movement written by Germaine Greer – a public intellectual imbued with immense self-confidence – women were stimulated to think beyond social conditioning. Subsequently, they symbolically (and literally) dispensed with objects of oppression including mops, lipsticks, high heels (and bras) in their bid for freedom and empowerment. They agreed with Greer that their previous habit of being too polite, too nice, too deferential (and basically too afraid) to speak openly about important matters detracted from the creative energies necessary for self-fulfilment, choosing instead to act fearlessly.

Your point of view is important but not everyone has to agree. You can research facts and listen to each side of an argument but it takes strength to speak against the prevailing narrative, especially these days when coming from media 'influencers'. Conformity is easier, especially if you're unaware of the efficient propaganda that programs your views and behaviours.

Milgrim Experiments and Obeying Authority

The famous Milgram experiments of the 1960s[17] demonstrated how we are pre-programmed to act despite our expectations. The Milgram study measured the willingness of participants to obey an authority figure who instructed them to perform acts conflicting with their personal conscience. Participants were led to believe that they were administering electric shocks to a 'learner'. A very high proportion of subjects fully obeyed instructions.

Concerningly, they continued to increase the (fake) voltage to levels that would have been fatal had they been real. This propensity to obey authority figures is a behavioural science strategy used to exploit the susceptible and convince a population to follow particular rules. This is especially the case if endorsed by healthcare professionals or celebrity figures, yet they are instructed on what to say.

If you find yourself thinking your issues are insurmountable it's understandable that you're vulnerable to propaganda without realising that you've relinquished control. Situations promulgated by propagandists lead you to believe you have no control. It's likely that, as participants in the Milgram experiment demonstrated, you have been programmed to follow orders.

It takes enormous courage to stand up against propaganda in any form, whether from big business, big government, the media or your peers. When something is accepted by the majority, it's difficult even for the most confident to face the potential loneliness of railing against what everyone else is saying.

Adopting a controversial perspective is daunting so fear may induce you to grimly adhere to orders. Your gut tells you when something isn't right. If you feel uncomfortable, chances are you're being pressured but it's difficult to take an alternative view when you know you risk being rejected or ostracised if you don't follow the crowd.

For example, the majority accepted the importance of formerly behind-the-scenes bureaucrats as they constantly bombarded us with rhetoric about pandemics, vaccines and COVID-19. The media endorsed the authority's draconian measures to control the population. Worldwide, the majority complied with the demands. Few were prepared to lose their jobs, to be precluded from attending workplaces, universities and social events, thus they ignored any doubts about the experimental mRNA injections and had them anyway.

Those who withstood the coercive practices paid a high price for their resistance. Journalists were suppressed from suggesting that the SARS-CoV-2 was likely to be no worse than a bad seasonal flu or demonised as anti-Chinese racists if they said that it came from a laboratory. Individuals suspicious of the Warp Speed timeline for developing a mRNA vaccine program were mocked.

Confident Rebellion

A brave nurse who lost her job at a hospital because she refused an mRNA vaccine explained her struggle to uphold her views when the authorities pressured her to conform. Speaking to a large audience she explained that, because of what she had seen as a nurse she would not stay silent. She said:

'The [COVID vaccine] adverse reactions are catastrophic. There are thousands of them. There are heart attacks, people having limbs removed as a result of blood clots, an increased number of stillborn babies, babies born with all kinds of horrendous ... [she loses her breath]. Cancer is on the rise. People who have been in remission from cancer are now having it return with a vengeance [since being injected]. And it [the injection] is NOT a vaccine. We have so many adverse reactions.'

Her confidence intact, she left the profession she'd loved her whole life and re-trained as a natural health practitioner.

Other professionals shared similar stories. Teachers left their workplaces to establish home-schooling practices. Doctors and other health professionals, unable to comply with commands issued by their registration body, left the profession but were vilified. Relationships between colleagues, friends and family fractured.

Maybe you're among the confident few who've challenged a prevailing narrative. Hopefully, you've not suffered, as did a young pregnant mother who tried to organise a protest march against the lockdowns in Victoria and was arrested in front of her children while still in her pyjamas.

Activism requires supreme confidence and tenacity. Contemporary protesters on university campuses and participants in large city uprisings, together with worldwide farmers and other protesters, work together to spread information about government over-reach.

You don't have to be as famous as Galileo, the Italian astronomer, arrested for being suspected of heresy who has subsequently been known as 'the father of modern science'[18] to challenge the prevailing narrative. You don't have to be as strong as Rosa Parks, arrested for not vacating her seat to a white man, whose actions spawned a civil rights movement in the USA. Nor do you need to be as controversial or stand out like Nelson Mandela, who despite being jailed for challenging apartheid, went on to become the first president of South Africa in order to demonstrate individuality and confidence.

Once in possession of the facts, you can make informed decisions. It's when you're not well-versed about an issue that fear of the unknown can create stress. For example, how many understand the implications of belonging to bodies such as the United Nations (UN) with its global warming rhetoric embedded in AGENDA 21 (A21) and yet it impacts us all? Or who knew that former deputy prime minister, the Hon. Julie Bishop MP, committed Australia's support for the UN protection of the world's environment by controlling all people and resources once countries transfer political power and finance to them?[19]

Maybe you're one of the educated few aware of this reorientation of society and the worldwide redeployment of human and financial resources, including renewable energy and investment in energy infrastructure associated with redeploying wealth. It's now known as Agenda 2030 and refers to eating meat, consuming fossil fuels, owning motor vehicles, working and living in air-conditioning as not sustainable .

Increasing costs and responsibilities can be overwhelming, leaving you with little time to think about issues such as changes in society. It may seem easier to focus on things you can change such as your body, health and relationships, rather than worry about a sustainable development agenda or rhetoric about inclusive, fair societies.

Ageing can elicit greater clarity and the confidence to speak your mind. Some of my older clients are particularly confident, saying that as they have fewer years to live, they don't worry about what other people think. They confidently discuss big and small issues including government control over water allocation, building restrictions, what food we eat, the corrosion of rights, the economy, education and the future of their grandchildren. They also use social media to vent their frustrations.

Others, like Melanie, are more focussed on their failed marriages and the loss of their professional careers due to a past stance they took about injections rather than the potential impact of future events or government policy.

Melanie Rebuilds Her Confidence

Melanie lost her job because she had stood against the vaccine mandates. She was also rejected by her husband for her stance over the injections. After two failed marriages, she had trust issues and engaged in a bitter fight with her ex-husband in order to profit from the sale of their property. She then focussed on her appearance with continual enhancements in her desperate attempt to find love.

She lost sight of her chronological age as she constantly battled with her body, working out at gyms, meeting bodybuilders and pretending to be their age in the hope of a relationship. Melanie had hair extensions to establish long blonde tresses and she bought every procedure she could afford to change her shape. But no procedures helped her overcome her trust issues.

She only felt comfortable in the company of an overweight man more than 20 years her senior, who was unvaccinated and accepting of her temperament. She was hostile, blamed the system, her former colleagues and her ex-husband, and denigrated the family members who had abandoned her because of the stance she took.

Her social world shrunk to the extent that the only person in whose company she would spend time was the older father-figure. She rang him morning, noon and night and accepted invitations to coffee. He was flattered by her attention, especially as she was a much younger woman with a physically fit body. She flaunted herself in front of males and females when in public places but it was clear from her conversation that she was uncomfortable with people her own age.

Her father-figure also lacked confidence. His only other friends were the shopkeepers and wait staff at the cafes they frequented. Subsequently, he received vicarious pleasure when she joined him because her body and overtly sexualised mannerisms drew attentive looks from other customers. She knew he enjoyed the attention, so she played on his devotion. Having coffee with him suited them both, as they were both insecure and needy. Because he listened to her, she felt temporarily reassured that she was of value to someone.

Despite her continual presence in the older man's life, it wasn't enough to sustain Melanie's well-being in the long-term. At her doctor's suggestion, she agreed to try therapy. Coincidentally, once she'd made the first appointment, she was also approached to join a company offering the same line of work as her previous employment. She had an interview and a new job and she also attended therapy and began to understand herself.

Once she was established at work and her house settlement was completed, Melanie's hostility and excessive focus on her appearance diminished. She began to enjoy working and socialising with colleagues in her own age group again. She let go of her negativity and found like-minded colleagues. As she got to know others and shared their stories, she became more confident and began to speak her mind, but her confidence was still fragile.

Her apprehension returned when it was revealed that former friends and family members had developed serious health conditions, and/or had died suddenly. Instead of worrying about her looks, these anecdotes began to preoccupy her. She embarked on intensive research.

Her doctor confided that she was overwhelmed at the rise in cancers, and especially concerned at the reappearance of cancers among her many patients whom she'd considered cured but who were now finding suddenly that they were no longer in remission. Melanie's confidence was buoyed by being honoured that her doctor would confide in her. But she was also troubled thinking about her nieces when the doctor mentioned that organs, including the ovaries, could be adversely impacted.

Melanie had a new focus. She wanted it acknowledged among her old and new circles of friends and acquaintances that the injections could have accelerated an underlying medical condition, created a new medical condition, or resulted in the recently labelled mysterious Sudden Adult Death (SAD).

Melanie was aware that she could be dismissed for providing false or misleading information but she was steadfast in her views that mRNA vaccines should be withdrawn from the market so she discussed it only with the few people who shared her views. They'd learnt that giving false or misleading Information is an offence 'under section 307B of the Crimes Act 1900, which carries a maximum penalty of 2 years in prison'[20] and Melanie had no intention of losing her newly regained confidence.

Given the limitations on freedom of speech, she was determined not to jeopardise her new employment by asking questions despite the reports of athletes, celebrities and other high-profile figures dying in record numbers post-vaccine roll out. She monitored her speech and with whom she said what she thought so as not to diminish her newly regained confidence.

She felt free to remark about overt commentaries, and she shared Senator Gerrad Rennick's showcase of stories about Australians suffering from COVID-19 injuries. She agreed with his writing on social media (info@gerardrennick.com.au) and his thoughts that, as part of today's world exists in a state of war against terrorism, we need the freedom to talk and discuss events if we're to be confident in our government and our own roles.

Melanie told her friends, 'It is incumbent on you to at least explore how adherence to instructions about behaviour matches your principles and values regardless of threats.' She was heartened that her friends who'd previously denigrated those who refused to follow edicts, after noticing heart attacks in previously fit athletes, no longer normalised myocarditis as if it was common. They also commented on the placement of defibrillator machines everywhere and the nomenclature of the growing numbers of sudden deaths in previously healthy adults post-vaccination as Sudden Adult Death (SAD) syndrome.

They agreed that advertisements presenting strokes in children as the new normal were weird. Many of them knew someone who was ill, who'd died from sudden stage four cancers or who reported unexplained bleeding and/or heart, lung or neurological complications. Melanie was reassured by her friends that, as alarm bells rang for them, many began to change to her point of view.

Social media includes many stories of those who report a change of heart. The pandemic has passed, but a type of lockdown amnesia and fear, which erodes confidence, has affected others.

No one willingly believes that their government would dupe an entire population or that they would be complicit in punishing colleagues, family members and peers who stand against the prevailing narrative. But a look back through novels, including *Nineteen Eighty-Four,* reveals tests applied that go against normal people's thinking.

In that novel, the main character's job was to shove inconvenient facts down a memory hole so that the masses would forget them. But it's not 1984. Evidence that the vaccines and procedures imposed on the populations were more problematic than useful now flows from many quarters.

Faith and trust in our institutions, the government, the media and our health practitioners' response to COVID-19 tested many people's confidence. Perhaps an unintended consequence is that it has seen people of all ages collectively gaining confidence about their health status, what they will tolerate from the workplace, governments and employers, and building on their ability to withstand propaganda, bullying or harassment. Even the negativity elicited by family or friends did not deter everyone. Young and old, like Melanie's friends, have become more self-confident to speak their minds.

You don't need to surrender to propaganda or anyone who tries to force you to act against your will. Once you grow in self-confidence, you won't buckle under the weight of any rules and regulations or pressures from the media or industry. A confident individual, you're nonetheless realistic enough to know that there will be situations whereby, when you feel fearful because everyone else is heading in a different direction, you'll choose discretion rather than confrontation.

As the Maslow hierarchy suggests, humans need to belong, so for optimum mental and physical health, surround yourself where possible with other like-minded souls. This enables you to reinforce your self-belief when all else points to the contrary, and remain confident in your value as a member of society. Looking inwards for reassurance helps you to repel any old negative influences that have been waiting to swallow you with their hyperbole from the past about your self-worth.

With confidence, you can withstand the negativity of family, teachers and others who seek to undermine you. Taking the example of JD Vance, Vice President to President Donald Trump in the United States of America (USA), we note that it's possible to run for one of the highest leadership positions in the world despite a childhood marked by poverty, neglect and surrounded by drugs and abuse.[21]

He pulled himself up from a life of helplessness by experiencing the care shown to him by his grandmother and sister, family loyalties and an innate ability that saw him study law at a prestigious university. He had a career in the Marines, a happy marriage and fatherhood, and became an author, a venture capitalist and now a politician and holder of one of the most important roles in the Western world. In Maslow's terms, it seems that he has adequately fulfilled all his needs.

The Reality of Treatment Costs

Once your basic needs are met, there is freedom to realise your higher purpose, which Maslow called self-actualisation. But propaganda works. Attacks on your self-assurance are a dream for advertisers . At times, anxiety and self-doubt – fodder for advertisers and businesses – affect even the most confident of us. Commercial advertisers and marketing companies are experts at working on vanity.

If you haven't yet reached your higher self and some situations have left you feeling unusually vulnerable, you're likely to yield when clever, subtle marketing pressures are applied. At the most basic level, fear about yourself is income generating for health food businesses, retreats, surgeons, other professionals including dentists, and the media.

Manufacturers and those spruiking various diet and food supplements cash in when you lack self-confidence and depend on you acceding to their messages. Even actresses such as Jane Fonda are vulnerable but then she monetised her knowledge about low self-image and introduced aerobic classes.

Worry about your image, under pressure, you may be tempted to make purchases you later regret, or having bought a gift voucher, feel obliged to continue the habit. Supposed bargains entice you to part with your money for something that will never be used.

If you decide to undertake surgery, you will be made aware of the huge costs. Better and cheaper to learn to live with and appreciate yourself. If you find your purpose and focus on aspects beyond yourself can help make a better world and can lead to a meaningful and richer life.

When you believe in yourself the world is your oyster. It's possible to make massive plans, such as travelling in space or flying non-stop around the world. Alternatively, you can simplify your life and discover that observing the natural beauty of a landscape is the most fulfilling and rewarding thing you wish for.

Chapter Ten

We can't all be powerful leaders such as the Vice President of the USA or represent a symbol of peace such as the Dalai Lama. We can expect that, as we live in a prosperous nation, based on the understanding that hard work is rewarded, we are relatively free.

We're still influenced by mainstream television and printed newspapers, as well as the developments of our modern, affluent society. Nevertheless, despite all the medicines and efforts to keep humans alive, no one can go on for ever. The only certainty is that your time is finite. This realisation impacts all of us differently.

Paul Makes a Career Change at a Mature Age

Age is not equated to how well you cope. On reaching your mid-70s (the 'new 60s'), you may begin to worry that time is running out to do the things you want to accomplish. You can come to the end stage of your career and life with dreams unfulfilled or you can change at any age.

If you make confident choices, you continue your dreams with a renewed vigour for life. On a recent plane trip, cabin crew attendant Paul's chatter reinforced how easily it can happen.

Settled in my seat for the flight, I was drawn to the sounds of laughter emanating from the front of the plane. I couldn't see any reason for it and resumed my reading until a member of the cabin crew came down the aisle and stopped at the row behind me. Soon, the family in those seats were in an animated conversation with him and much hilarity ensued. Relaxed in my seat but intrigued, I overheard the conversation taking place behind me between the passengers and the cabin crew attendant.

Conversing about their onward flight, the travellers referred to him as Paul. It became apparent that they were to holiday in Greece and he made suggestions about places they could visit. I'd enjoyed magnificent holidays myself in Greece so I was captivated by their conversation. Amid their lively banter about Greece, Paul revealed that he had been a pharmacist for most of his life and had only, as a mature man, obtained the cabin crew job four months previously. He recounted how much he loved his new role.

Amongst their snatches of conversation and merriment, I learnt more of his story. His mother had recently passed away so he no longer felt obliged to continue working as a pharmacist although he'd enjoyed many aspects of the work during his erstwhile lengthy career. It transpired that he'd also tended to his mother as her health failed in recent years. Once she was gone, he was sad that she was no longer in his life, but nevertheless felt liberated to retire from the pharmacy and pursue his lifelong dream.

He explained that he'd always had a passion for flying but felt constrained to follow a more traditional path to please his mother. Paul obviously loved to talk and stayed with the family chatting for many minutes until he had to return to the front of the aisle and participate in the safety demonstration. As he passed my row, I noted a man of mature years. I estimated him to be around 65 years of age.

The census reveals that many of us are over 65. It doesn't mean we have to give up work. There are ample stories like Paul's of people who have retired, only to find themselves once again in the workforce in a paid or voluntary capacity.

We can't all be like Paul, changing occupations and continuing to work infinitely. When it's time for retirement, we can embrace it. If it hasn't yet arrived for you, it could be time to let go of things that constrain your happiness and fulfilment. You don't have to wait until you've left work to be the person you always wanted to be.

You may find it easier when you're retired because you no longer worry about saying something that will affect your career. Unless you're like Paul. He was happy to speak about matters beyond the purview of his role because of his natural ebullience and lack of concern about security.

There are no limits associated with Confidage. Naturally, you follow the obligatory social norms and unwritten rules of conduct that preclude you from causing deliberate harm to another person by word or deed. Beyond that, the longer you live, the boundaries you face – for example worrying about what others will think of you – are self-induced.

Experienced, let your perspective and knowledge guide you as you express your thoughts and opinions. Act out of self-love for if you don't love yourself, how can you expect love from others? Feeling more self-assured at an older age, your confidence can still be thrown by unforeseen events, as was the case with Meredith.

Our Time is Finite

Meredith came to me distraught about her friend and colleague Dr Joe. She was a mature-aged woman who maintained her fitness as a yoga teacher. She confided that she was dating a well-loved general practitioner (GP) of a similar age. They'd discovered that they held similar views about life and the universe.

She'd learnt that Dr Joe was a diligent and much-loved GP of more than 40 years. When he revealed the concerns he shared with his national and international collegiate network about the pandemic, she was honoured that he respected her enough to share their findings.

At that same time, Meredith and her colleagues, researching the same issue, were more sceptical, so Meredith withheld conflicting doubts when Dr Joe kindly offered to place her high in the queue for the experimental vaccines. A quiet man, he never bragged to

Meredith about his achievements, including, as she learnt, that he'd topped his classes at school and university where he worked his way through medical school on a scholarship.

Invited to enter many specialities, he chose to remain 'in touch with grassroots patients', hence training for entry to the Royal Australian College of General Practitioners (RACGP).

Meredith observed his eager participation in the mass-vaccination program. After his first two injections, he insisted his loved ones follow suit, believing the rhetoric that it would keep them safe. The relationship blossomed but, due to their mutual respect for each other, Dr Joe accepted her polite refusal of his vaccine.

It was not long before he confessed his apprehension upon noticing a spike in vaccine injuries among his patients after the injections. She suggested he share his worries with colleagues, but none were willing to discuss it. Dr Joe's belief in vaccines was then sorely tested.

Dr Joe's confidence in his profession and the regulatory body was dashed. His own father, a formerly robust, fit 92-year-old, succumbed to a heart condition immediately after the first injection. His doubts reached the ear of the authorities and he was pressured to conform. He wouldn't comply so was immediately censored as the propaganda intensified.

Word of his father's rapid deterioration and Dr Joe's behaviour spread. Two medical specialist colleagues who shared his views approached him. Realising that he wasn't alone boosted his confidence and the three men formed an alliance. As they embarked on an intensive campaign of research, they received invitations to speak at gatherings with others, similarly angry at the system and accompanying huge financial rewards payable to drug companies. But the stress took its toll.

Before long, Dr Joe found he had inoperable cancer. Meredith was devastated that after all this time, now that they were officially an item, he was dying. This explained her visit to me. This blow completely undermined her resilience. Her usual coping strategies didn't help.

Her mood was very low, but she didn't want to add to Dr Joe's worries. Her bitterness and unusual negativity undermined her self-assurance. She was grief-stricken that, having found love at a mature age when she'd all but given up, the person to whom she'd become attached was fading away. The inner confidence she'd grown throughout her long career as a yoga teacher was sorely tested and she was filled with self-doubt.

Through our work, Meredith gradually recovered a constructive perspective. She changed the direction of her attention. Instead of entirely focussing on him, she was reassured that it was important to put herself and her needs back at the forefront of her picture.

Meredith was reminded of mindfully taking one day at a time without worrying about what lay ahead. Upon regaining her former joie de vie, she stopped worrying about Dr Joe's long-term prognosis, knowing no one can last forever. She planned small getaways for them between and following his treatments and re-organised her work so they could enjoy being together for as long as they could.

Ill health – your own, your partner's or even a friend's – can be extremely difficult although hopefully not as dire as Meredith's situation. Ageing brings forth many changes, but when combined with ill-health, lost love, changing relationships or death, it can throw you into a spin. However, there are always solutions – some great, some quite minor – with a constructive mindset.

If you have to limit or let go of work completely, like Dr Joe, but your sense of purpose has been linked to your career, the transition can exacerbate a loss of self-esteem. If you plan for change, as well as the unexpected, it helps when the time comes. Keep in contact with like-minded and age-related peers. Often, they are one and the same group, as Celie explained.

Celie: Acceptance at 70

She told her friends that she actually felt different once she acknowledged her 70th birthday. After fighting ageing and ignoring her birthdays as far as possible in the past, she confided that having reached 70, she no longer cared who knew her age. She felt relieved that she could relax.

After a lifetime of being and doing everything for others, she no longer felt selfish about taking time for herself. In the process, she relinquished the struggle to look younger and the pressure she'd been under to always prove her competence by helping everyone else and doing 'the right thing'.

Interestingly, Celie realised that the more relaxed she became, the more it rubbed off on her peers. She noticed some of her friends and colleagues adopting similar behaviours, commenting that she was their model. Family members also commented that now she exuded positive energy and was more enjoyable to be around. These positive remarks reinforced her self-confidence.

She gave up wearing uncomfortably high-heeled shoes and tight-fitting clothes, stopped pretending she liked parties or being with large groups of people, and avoided going anywhere after dark if she had to drive. Celie also started to take greater responsibility for her health, exercising more and cutting out processed foods. She began to reduce the stress in her life created by the conflicting demands of having two jobs, making time to be at home without working all the time. Some weekends she stayed at home alone and did no work at all.

Celie said her most important lesson was accepting, not fearing, the reality of death. Ceasing to worry about it, she started to plan for older age and for death itself. She thought a lot about the people she'd known who'd died in their youth or middle age, and many in their 70s. She felt lucky to be alive, still working and reasonably healthy.

Whilst she'd expected to outlive her parents who'd died in their late 80s, she accepted that it was not guaranteed. She acknowledged that her current life was nothing like when she was in her 50s. Nonetheless, she said it was equally precious.

'Life's a whole lot better with so much to do, the time to do it, and not trying to keep up appearances to please anyone else. I'm certainly not going to waste a moment of it pretending, especially to myself, that I'm 20 years younger.'

Celie had dealt with challenges at each new stage of life. Busy with work and raising a family in her 30s, she'd had no time to compare herself with others, yet due to a lack of confidence, that's precisely what she did. At 70, embracing her true self, she joyfully shared her happiness with friends and family.

Then she enlightened her social groups, including book club and tennis group members. She encouraged the lonely, those without children, family, work or health, or who had lost special people to 'age joyfully, wear what you like, eat and drink what you like within moderation, say whatever is on your mind and ditch fear'.

If, like Celie , you're preparing for the post-work stages or your family has left home and your thoughts have turned towards retirement and changes to your lifestyle, here are some more things to consider:

1. It's time to use and enjoy the money you saved up. You don't have to keep it to give to those who have no idea of the sacrifices you

made to get it. There's nothing worse than a son or daughter-in-law with big ideas for your hard-earned capital. **Warning:** This is not a time for making bad investments, even if they sound fool-proof. Nor is it time to worry. It's a time for you to enjoy some peace and quiet.

2. Stop worrying about your children and grandchildren's financial future. You've done your job, taking care of them and teaching them what you could. You provided education, food, shelter and support. It's their responsibility to earn an income and provide for their own family and your turn now.

3. Keep yourself healthy. No need to exert great physical effort. Do moderate exercise (like walking every day), eat well and get adequate sleep. It's easy to become sick but harder to remain healthy, so keep yourself in good shape. Be aware of your medical and physical needs, but don't be consumed by them. Keep in touch with your doctor and stay informed.

4. Always buy the best, most beautiful items for your significant other. The key goal is to enjoy your money with your partner. One day one of you will miss the other and the

money won't provide any comfort then, so enjoy it together.

5. Don't stress over the little things. You've already overcome so much in your life. You have good memories and bad ones, but the important thing is the present. Don't let the past drag you down and don't let the future frighten you. Feel good in the now. Small issues will soon be forgotten.

6. Regardless of age, always keep love alive. Love your partner, love life, love your family, love your neighbour and remember – you're not old as long as you have intelligence and someone (a person(s) and/or pet) who loves you.

7. Be proud, both inside and out. When you are well-maintained on the outside, it seeps in, making you feel proud and strong.

8. Don't lose sight of fashion trends for your age but keep your own sense of style. There's nothing worse than an older person trying to wear the current fashion of a younger generation. You can still have fun playing around with fashions and trends but having developed your own sense of what looks good on you, be proud of it. It's part of who you are.

9. Stay up-to-date. Go online and read what people are saying. Use email and social

networks to keep in touch with what's going on in the world at large as well as your immediate environment and the people you know.

10. Respect others and their opinions. Today's youth are the future, and none of us know what's ahead, so don't criticise those whose ideas differ from your own. You're never too old to learn from others.

11. Don't patronise by reminding the younger generation about what was like when you were younger. You can still find common ground with them while keeping in touch with your peers to share similar stories and help them understand conditions from your early life. Have fun and enjoy your present life and the people in it.

12. Life is too short to waste on bitterness and regret. You can reflect on and learn from the past but you can't change it. Spend time with positive, cheerful people and be grateful for something every day.

13. Don't live with your children or grandchildren if you have a financial choice. We all need our privacy. Visit and enjoy, being mindful of their needs, and keep your awareness of the differences between generations for your conversations with your peers.

14. Keep up with hobbies, new and old, or volunteer. Be your own detective, searching until you find something you like.

15. Even if you don't feel like it, accept invitations that get you out and about. It costs nothing to visit galleries and museums, walk on a beach or experience other aspects of nature. You can initiate a coffee date with friends or acquaintances or join a club.

16. Talk less and listen more. Be mindful of whether or not your listeners are really interested. Try to keep complaints to a minimum as people have a low tolerance for whinging. It's better to say something positive.

17. Don't dwell on pain and discomfort as you get older. It's a part of the cycle of life. Minimise them in your mind by reminding yourself that you're not pain, it's something additional to your life. Thus, you detract from focussing on a negative or uncomfortable situation.

18. If you've been offended by someone and have been holding on to the grudge, it's time to let it go. Resentment only makes you sad and bitter. It doesn't matter who was right. If you were in the wrong, apologise. You always have a choice – you can forgive

and forget, then move on with your life or remain stuck.

19. Don't waste your time trying to convince others to agree with your beliefs. They'll make their own choices no matter what you say. People believe what they want to, despite the evidence, for a variety of reasons. It's not your responsibility if they allow themselves to be misguided, but if you choose to share your perspectives and they don't agree, leave it alone otherwise you'll be left feeling frustrated. Better to model your beliefs and let your behaviour influence them.

20. Use humour. Laughing is a great source of stress relief. Laughter is used as therapy, to relieve pain and improve well-being. Laugh whenever you can. It feels so good to share.

21. Ignore what others say about you, especially if it is second-hand. You can't control what others will say about you so don't waste time thinking about what they might say or think.

Ageing is associated with life transitions and physical and social environments as well as personal characteristics such as sex, ethnicity or socioeconomic status. Realistically, some complex health states occur in later life but there's no typical older person. Maybe you remember when your shy grandma changed, opening up and speaking about things whereas she'd previously kept quiet as she was 70 or 80. Many 80-year-olds' physical and mental capacities haven't changed, whereas others decline at a much younger age.

Gradually decreasing physical and mental capacity is neither linear nor consistent, and only loosely associated with your age. Confident people recognise that success and acceptance aren't achieved because of maintaining an eternally youthful appearance nor is it reserved for the young.

Outward manifestations of self-assurance based on boasting or arrogance are unattractive at any age. While you may have avoided these people in the past now you understand that keeping up with appearances is their way to hide unhappiness. As shown in the many stories here, we don't necessarily know their full story.

As demonstrated, a Confidage approach directs your attention to respect ageing. Confidently, you accept the impact of genetics, environment, chronological age and stage of life but most importantly you know how helpful thinking influences your feelings. You know your limitations but choose to flourish by focussing on your skills and strengths. If, after all, you have decided to opt for changes to your fitness, eating habits, work, fashions, location, living arrangements, lifestyle, friendship circles and more, just do it. Go ahead.

REMEMBER: 'Life is too short to drink bad wine.'

REFERENCES

Chapter 2

1 'Australia's spend on cosmetic treatments tops $1 billion', Cosmetics Physicians College of Australasia, https://cpca.net.au/australias-spend-on-cosmetic-treatments-tops-1-billion-2/

2 'Celebrity Botched Up Bodies', https://www.dailymotion.com/video/x449dun

3 'Assaults on emergency workers', Victoria Police, *Herald Sun* 14 August 2023 from https://www.heraldsun.com.au › news-story

4 'What's normal (and what's not) as you age', retrieved online from *Webmd.com*, https://www.webmd.com/healthy-aging/story/what-to-expect-aging#:~:text=It's%20no%20secret%20your%20mind,work%20a%20little%20less%20well

5 'The world's fastest-ageing societies', *The Gold Coast Bulletin*, 17 September 2024, p. 3.

Chapter 3

6 'The generations defined', https://mccrindle.com.au/article/topic/demographics/the-generations-defined/

Chapter 4

7   7. 'School installs litter boxes and promises more cat-friendly policies after increase in 'feline-identifying' students', *Damascus Drop Bear*, 22 August 2022, https://damascusdropbear.com.au/school-installs-litter-boxes-and-promises-more-cat-friendly-policies-after-increase-in-feline-identifying-students/

Chapter 5

8   8. 'Homeland truths unspoken' by Jacinta Price, *The West Australian*, 12 August 2016, https://thewest.com.au/news/australia/homeland-truths-unspoken-ng-ya-115337

9   9. '8 Celebs Who Unexpectedly Opened Up About Their Insecurities and Made Us Love Them Even More', *Bright Side*, https://brightside.me/articles/7-celebrities-who-struggled-with-low-self-esteem-show-us-were-not-alone-805619/

10 Lifeline Australia, Crisis Support, call 13 11 14 or use chat or text 0477 13 11 14 for 24/7 crisis support, https://www.lifeline.org.au

11 Beyond Blue, 24/7 Support for Anxiety, Depression and Anxiety, call 1300 22 4636, https://www.beyondblue.org.au

Chapter 7

12 'Older Australians', *Australian Institute of Health and Welfare*, updated on 2 July 2024, https://www.aihw.gov.au/reports/older-people/older-australians/contents/health/health-disability-status

Chapter 8

13 'Maslow's hierarchy of needs', *Wikipedia*, https://en.wikipedia.org/wiki/Maslow%27s_hierarchy_of_needs

14 Mavrodaris A, Mattocks C, Brayne CE. 'Healthy ageing for a healthy planet: Do sustainable solutions exist?' (2021). *The Lancet*, Jan, 2(1): e10-e11. https://www.thelancet.com/journals/lanhl/article/PIIS2666-7568(20)30067-2/fulltext

15 'What's normal (and what's not) as you age', retrieved online from *Webmd.com*, https://www.webmd.com/healthy-aging/story/what-to-expect-aging#:~:text=It's%20no%20secret%20your%20mind,work%20a%20little%20less%20well

Chapter 9

16 Greer G, *The Female Eunuch*, 1970. HarperCollins, UK.

17 Vaughan, G, Hogg, M. *Introduction to Social Psychology*, 1995. Prentice Hall, pp 124-127.

18 'Galileo Galilei', *History.com*, retrieved 30 September 2024, https://www.history.com/topics/inventions/galileo-galilei

19 Lennon, S, *The Sustainable Development Goals and Australia – A National and Personal Roadmap to Sustainability*, 27 September 2015 (Extracts), United Nations Association of Australia. https://www.unaa.org.au/wp-content/uploads/2017/04/WA_UN_SDGsAndAustralia.pdf

20 CRIMES ACT 1900 – SECT 307B False or misleading information and penalties, http://classic.austlii.edu.au › nsw › ca190082 › s307b

21 Vance, J.D. *Hillbilly Elegy: A Memoir of a Family and Culture in Crisis*, 2017, Farmington Hills, Mich: Thorndike Press.

Kantor, JH, 'Top 10 People Who Changed The World By Breaking The Rules', Listverse, https://listverse.com/2021/04/27/top-10-people-who-changed-the-world-by-breaking-the-rules/

'The Evolution of Female Body Image Ideals', *Dietetically Speaking*, 19 July 2021, https://dieteticallyspeaking.com/the-evolution-of-female-body-image-ideals/#:~:text=The%201960s,an%20adolescent%20physique%20(8)

ABOUT THE AUTHOR

Dr Sallie Gardner has 25 years' experience as a developmental psychologist, working with a diverse range of clients across a broad spectrum of ages, including children, adolescents, adults and seniors. She holds a PhD in the area of psychological distress. Her forte is in using her training as a psychologist, educator and counsellor to communicate well-being strategies, help clients overcome fears, particularly in relation to ageing, and enhance confidence across the lifespan.

www.ingramcontent.com/pod-product-compliance
Lightning Source LLC
Chambersburg PA
CBHW022220090526
44585CB00013BB/561